ClearRevise®

OCR Cambridge Nationals
Sport Science

Illustrated revision and practice

Levels 1/2
J828 (R180)

Reducing the risk of sports injuries and dealing with common medical conditions

Published by
PG Online Limited
The Old Coach House
35 Main Road
Tolpuddle
Dorset
DT2 7EW
United Kingdom

sales@pgonline.co.uk
www.clearrevise.com
www.pgonline.co.uk
2024

PG ONLINE

PREFACE

Absolute clarity! That's the aim.

This is everything you need to ace the examined components in this course and beam with pride. Each topic is laid out in a beautifully illustrated format that is clear, approachable and as concise and simple as possible.

Each section of the Sport Science R180 specification is clearly indicated to help you cross-reference your revision. The checklist on the contents pages will help you keep track of what you have already worked through and what's left before the big day.

We have included worked exam-style questions with answers for almost every topic. This helps you understand where marks are coming from and to see the theory at work for yourself in an exam situation. There is also a set of exam-style questions at the end of each section for you to practise writing answers for. You can check your answers against those given at the end of the book.

LEVELS OF LEARNING

Based on the degree to which you are able to truly understand a new topic, we recommend that you work in stages. Start by reading a short explanation of something, then try and recall what you've just read. This has limited effect if you stop there but it aids the next stage. Question everything. Write down your own summary and then complete and mark a related exam-style question. Cover up the answers if necessary but learn from them once you've seen them. Lastly, teach someone else. Explain the topic in a way that they can understand. Have a go at the different practice questions – they offer an insight into how and where marks are awarded.

ACKNOWLEDGMENTS

The questions in this ClearRevise guide are the sole responsibility of the authors and have neither been provided nor approved by the examination board.

Every effort has been made to trace and acknowledge ownership of copyright. The publishers will be happy to make any future amendments with copyright owners that it has not been possible to contact. The publisher would like to thank the following companies and individuals who granted permission for the use of their images in this textbook.

All Sections

Photographic images: © Shutterstock
Rugby tackle © News Images LTD / Alamy Stock Photo
Zinedine Zidane © ph.FAB / Shutterstock
Owen Farrell © Marco Iacobucci Epp / Shutterstock

Rugby game injury treatment © A_Lesik / Shutterstock
Christian Eriksen © Marco Iacobucci Epp / Shutterstock
Ethan Dick © Alex Bogatyrev / Shutterstock
Charlie Wi © Chatchai Somwat / Shutterstock

Design and artwork: PG Online Ltd
First edition 2024   10 9 8 7 6 5 4 3 2 1
A catalogue entry for this book is available from the British Library
ISBN: 978-1-916518-10-0

Contributor: Anthony Liddle
Copyright © PG Online 2024
All rights reserved

No part of this publication may be reproduced, stored in a retrieval system, or transmitted in any form or by any means without the prior written permission of the copyright owner.

This product is made of material from well-managed FSC®-certified forests and from recycled materials.

Printed by Bell and Bain Ltd, Glasgow, UK.

THE SCIENCE OF REVISION

Illustrations and words

Research has shown that revising with words and pictures doubles the quality of responses by students.[1] This is known as 'dual-coding' because it provides two ways of fetching the information from our brain. The improvement in responses is particularly apparent in students when they are asked to apply their knowledge to different problems. Recall, application and judgement are all specifically and carefully assessed in public examination questions.

Retrieval of information

Retrieval practice encourages students to come up with answers to questions.[2] The closer the question is to one you might see in a real examination, the better. Also, the closer the environment in which a student revises is to the 'examination environment', the better. Students who had a test 2–7 days away did 30% better using retrieval practice than students who simply read, or repeatedly reread material. Students who were expected to teach the content to someone else after their revision period did better still.[3] What was found to be most interesting in other studies is that students using retrieval methods and testing for revision were also more resilient to the introduction of stress.[4]

Ebbinghaus' forgetting curve and spaced learning

Ebbinghaus' 140-year-old study examined the rate at which we forget things over time. The findings still hold true. However, the act of forgetting facts and techniques and relearning them is what cements them into the brain.[5] Spacing out revision is more effective than cramming – we know that, but students should also know that the space between revisiting material should vary depending on how far away the examination is. A cyclical approach is required. An examination 12 months away necessitates revisiting covered material about once a month. A test in 30 days should have topics revisited every 3 days – intervals of roughly a tenth of the time available.[6]

Summary

Students: the more tests and past questions you do, in an environment as close to examination conditions as possible, the better you are likely to perform on the day. If you prefer to listen to music while you revise, tunes without lyrics will be far less detrimental to your memory and retention. Silence is most effective.[5] If you choose to study with friends, choose carefully – effort is contagious.[7]

---

1. Mayer, R. E., & Anderson, R. B. (1991). Animations need narrations: An experimental test of dual-coding hypothesis. *Journal of Education Psychology*, (83)4, 484–490.
2. Roediger III, H. L., & Karpicke, J.D. (2006). Test-enhanced learning: Taking memory tests improves long-term retention. *Psychological Science*, 17(3), 249–255.
3. Nestojko, J., Bui, D., Kornell, N. & Bjork, E. (2014). Expecting to teach enhances learning and organisation of knowledge in free recall of text passages. *Memory and Cognition*, 42(7), 1038–1048.
4. Smith, A. M., Floerke, V. A., & Thomas, A. K. (2016) Retrieval practice protects memory against acute stress. *Science*, 354(6315), 1046–1048.
5. Perham, N., & Currie, H. (2014). Does listening to preferred music improve comprehension performance? *Applied Cognitive Psychology*, 28(2), 279–284.
6. Cepeda, N. J., Vul, E., Rohrer, D., Wixted, J. T. & Pashler, H. (2008). Spacing effects in learning a temporal ridgeline of optimal retention. *Psychological Science*, 19(11), 1095–1102.
7. Busch, B. & Watson, E. (2019), *The Science of Learning*, 1st ed. Routledge.

CONTENTS AND CHECKLIST

R180: Reducing the risk of sports injuries and dealing with common medical conditions

Topic Area 1 Different factors which influence the risk and severity of injury

Specification point			☑
1.1	Extrinsic factors	2	☐
1.1.2	Coaching, instructing and leading	4	☐
1.1.3	Environment	6	☐
1.1.4	Equipment	8	☐
1.2.1	Intrinsic factors	10	☐
1.2.2	Psychological factors	12	☐
1.2.2–1.2.3	Aggression	14	☐
1.2.4	Mental strategies	16	☐
	Examination practice: Topic area 1	17	☐

Topic Area 2 Warm up and cool down routines

Specification point			☑
2.1	Key components of a warm up	18	☐
2.2.1	Physiological benefits of a warm up	20	☐
2.2.2	Psychological benefits of a warm up	22	☐
2.3	Key components of a cool down	24	☐
2.4	Physiological benefits of a cool down	26	☐
	Examination practice: Topic area 2	28	☐

Topic Area 3 Different types and causes of sports injuries

Specification point			☑
3.1.1	Acute injuries	29	☐
3.1.2	Soft tissue and hard tissue injuries	30	☐
3.1.3–3.1.4	Strains and sprains	31	☐
3.1.5	Skin damage	32	☐
3.1.6–3.1.7	Fractures and dislocations	34	☐
3.1.8	Head injuries	35	☐
3.2.1	Chronic injuries	36	☐
3.2.2	Tendonitis	38	☐
3.2.3	Epicondylitis	39	☐
3.2.4–3.2.5	Shin splints and stress fractures	40	☐
	Examination practice: Topic area 3	41	☐

Topic Area 4 — Reducing risk, treatment and rehabilitation of sports injuries and medical conditions

Specification point ☑

4.1.1	Safety checks	42 ☐
4.1.2	Strategies to help reduce the risk of sports injuries and medical conditions	44 ☐
4.1.3	Emergency Action Plans (EAP)	45 ☐
4.2.1	SALTAPS on-field assessment routine	46 ☐
4.2.2	DRABC	47 ☐
4.2.3	Recovery position	48 ☐
4.2.4	PRICE therapy	49 ☐
4.2.5	Use of X-rays to detect injury	50 ☐
4.2.6–4.2.7	Overview of treatments and therapies	51 ☐
4.2	Responses and treatment overview	52 ☐
	Examination practice: Topic area 4	54 ☐

Topic Area 5 — Causes, symptoms and treatment of medical conditions

Specification point ☑

5.1	Asthma	56 ☐
5.2	Diabetes	58 ☐
5.3	Epilepsy	60 ☐
5.4	Sudden Cardiac Arrest (SCA)	62 ☐
5.5.1–5.5.4	Hypothermia	64 ☐
5.5.5–5.5.8	Heat exhaustion	66 ☐
5.5.9–5.5.12	Dehydration	68 ☐
	Examination practice: Topic area 5	70 ☐

R181: Applying the principles of training: fitness and how it affects skill performance

Task 1	Components of fitness applied in sport	74 ☐
Task 2	Components of fitness applied in sport	75 ☐
Task 3	Apply principles of training in sport	75 ☐
Task 4	Organising and planning a fitness training programme	76 ☐
Task 5	Review own performance in planning and delivery of a fitness training programme	76 ☐
	Examination practice answers	77 ☐
	Levels-based mark scheme for extended response questions	82 ☐
	Index	84 ☐
	Examination tips	85 ☐

COMMAND VERBS

The exam paper will use the following command verbs in each question.

You may understand lots about a topic, but if you do not answer each question in the correct way, the mark you receive may be very low.

Study each of the command verbs below along with their meanings and how they are used to answer a question.

Analyse / Discuss

1. Separate or break down information into parts and identify their characteristics or elements.
2. Explain the pros and cons of a topic or argument and make reasoned comments.
3. Explain the impacts of actions using a logical chain of reasoning.

Use full paragraphs.

The full answer will usually be around a page of text.

The risk of injuries and medical conditions in sport is ever present.

Analyse the strategies used to help reduce the risk of sports injuries and medical conditions. [8]

---

1) One strategy to reduce risk is an athlete medical.
2) A medical is an examination by a doctor to assess an athlete's physical health and fitness levels.
3) Regular medical evaluations can help detect early signs and symptoms of specific medical conditions, such as diabetes, for early intervention, thereby reducing the impact on the athlete.

⭐ The exemplar answer given is only a guide with a single point. Your response should be more detailed, with more examples to support your judgments.

Choose or Circle

Select an answer from an option given.

Which **one** of the following is **not** an extrinsic factor of injury risk? [1]

A Coaching ☐
B Environment ☐
C Equipment ☐
D Technique ☑

Compare and contrast

Give an account of the similarities and differences between two or more items or situations.

Compare and contrast an open fracture and a closed fracture. [2]

Both fractures involve a broken bone from an impact injury. (Compare = 1) However, the bone pierces the skin in an open fracture, but does not pierce the skin in a closed fracture. (Contrast = 1)

Complete / Fill in

Add all the required or appropriate parts.

Add information, for example, to a table, diagram, or graph until it is final.

Complete **Table 1** by identifying **two** other individual variables that are classed as intrinsic factors to potential injury. [2]

Table 1

	Individual variables	
	Gender	
(i)	*Age*	(1)
	Experience	
(ii)	*Weight*	(1)

Describe

Give an account including all the relevant characteristics, qualities, or events.

You do not need to include a justification or reason.

Describe what is meant by anxiety. [2]

Anxiety is a negative emotional state,[1] *that is characterised by apprehension and fear.*[1]

Explain

An explain question needs **two** parts:

1. Give reasons for and / or causes of.
2. Give a linked explanation of why this example answers the question.

Use words or phrases such as 'because', 'therefore' or 'this means that' in your answer.

A comprehensive warm up before physical exercise can have several psychological benefits to an athlete.

Explain **one** psychological benefit of a warm up. [2]

Completing a warm up can boost motivation by signalling the start of physical activity.
(Reason = 1)
Therefore, intensifying the drive to perform well and encouraging greater effort.
(Linked explanation = 1)

Identify / State / Outline

Give factors or features.

Give short, factual answers.

Identify **one** hard tissue injury. [1]

Dislocation.[1]

Evaluate / Justify

Make a reasoned qualitative judgement considering different factors and using available knowledge / experience.

1. Write down all the factors or events that apply to a given context.
2. Consider the strengths and weaknesses of each.
3. Identify those that are most important.
4. Give a reasoned conclusion supported by evidence.

You should use full paragraphs to answer these questions.

The full answer will usually be around a page of text.

The PRICE therapy is a treatment method for acute sporting injuries.

It is commonly applied when dealing with soft tissue injuries.

Evaluate the use of PRICE therapy for a soft tissue injury. [8]

---

1) PRICE is an acronym for Protection, Rest, Ice, Compress and Elevate commonly used in the management of acute sporting injuries such as sprains and strains.

2) One benefit of applying ice to an injured area is to help reduce pain, swelling and inflammation associated with acute injuries. However, ice may not always be available.

3) I believe the ice component in PRICE therapy is most relevant as it causes blood vessels to constrict or narrow, reducing blood flow to the injured area, reducing swelling and bruising.

4) In conclusion, although all stages of the PRICE therapy are needed, the ice stage stands out for its ability to numb pain and act as an anti-inflammatory.

> ⭐ The exemplar answer given is only a guide, your response should be more detailed, with more examples to support your judgments.

Draw / Create / Annotate / Label

Add information to a table, diagram or graph.

Figure 1 shows the heart rate of an runner pre- and post exercise.

Label the warm up and cool down phases of activity. [2]

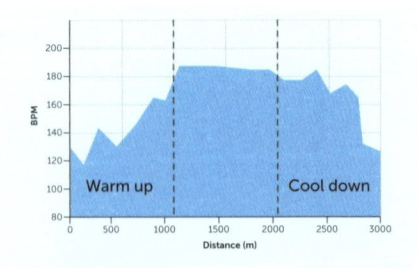

(Graph: BPM vs Distance (m), showing heart rate curve with "Warm up" labelled around 1000m and "Cool down" labelled around 2000–2500m.)

MARK ALLOCATIONS

Green mark allocations[1] on answers to in-text questions throughout this guide help to indicate where marks are gained within the answers. A bracketed '1' e.g. [1] = one valid point worthy of a mark. In longer answer questions, a mark is given based on the whole response. In these answers, a tick mark [✓] indicates that a valid point has been made. For a mark, a judgement should be made using the levels-based mark scheme on **page 82**. There are often many more points to make than there are marks available so you have more opportunity to max out your answers than you may think.

TOPICS FOR THE EXAM

Unit R180: Reducing the risk of sports injuries and dealing with common medical conditions

Information about the externally assessed exam:

Specification coverage

The importance of fitness for sports performance, fitness testing to determine fitness levels, and different fitness training methods.

The content for this assessment will be drawn from the essential subject content in sections A to D of Component 3 in the specification.

Assessment
Written exam: 75 minutes
70 marks
All questions are mandatory
40% of the qualification grade

Questions
A mix of short answer and longer answer questions assessing knowledge, understanding and skills in contextual scenarios building on all components within the qualification.

1.1
EXTRINSIC FACTORS

Extrinsic factors are those external to the body, that influence injury risk and severity. They include the type of activity, coaching quality, environment and equipment. Understanding these external influences is vital for athlete safety.

Types of sports activity

Certain sports and activities carry a higher level of risk compared to others, making it more likely that injuries may occur. Sports can be broadly categorised into contact and non-contact activities, each presenting different challenges and risks. A **contact** sport such as ice hockey, carries a greater risk of injury compared to a **non-contact** sport such as table tennis. The types and severity of injuries will differ substantially between the two.

> Compare with intrinsic factors on **page 10**.

Contact sports

Contact sports involve direct physical interactions between athletes and opponents, increasing the likelihood of injuries due to collisions, tackles and confrontations. For instance, in rugby, where players engage in forceful tackles and body checks, the risk of acute injuries such as fractures, sprains, and concussions (see **page 30–35**) are significantly increased. The sheer physicality of contact sports often leads to a higher severity of injuries.

Non-contact sports

Non-contact sports feature minimal physical interactions between athletes, reducing the risk of injuries caused by direct confrontations. Sports including tennis or swimming fall into this category, where athletes primarily engage in controlled and repetitive movements. While the risk of acute injuries (**page 29**) is generally lower in non-contact sports, there is an increased likelihood of overuse injuries (**page 36**). Chronic conditions such as stress fractures, tendonitis or muscle strains can develop owing to the repetitive nature of movements and the strain on specific muscle groups over time. The severity of these injuries is often related to the cumulative impact of repetitive actions rather than immediate physical confrontations.

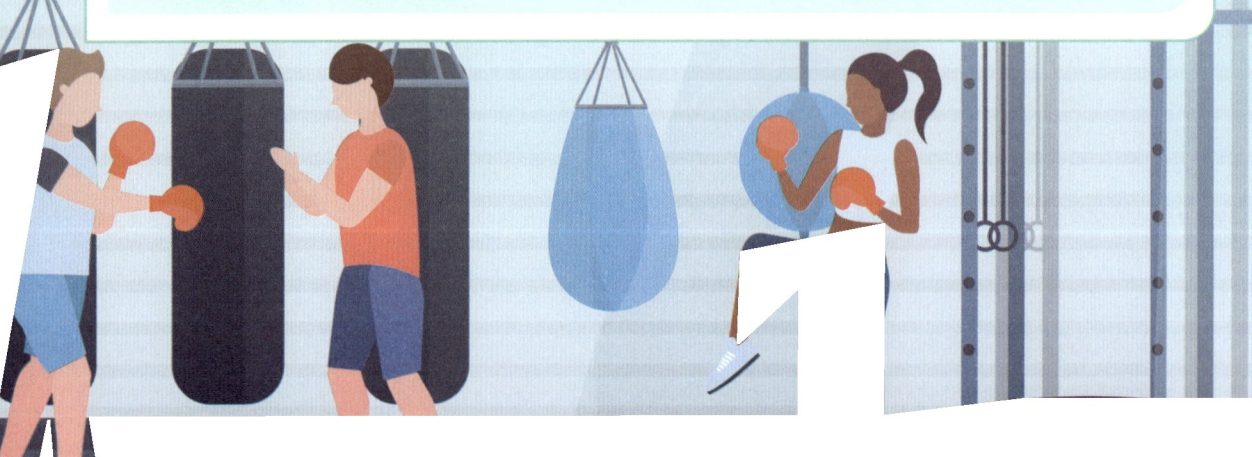

How different sporting activities can influence types of injury

Sporting activity	Common injuries	How the injury may occur
Contact sports (rugby)	Concussions, fractures, sprains, dislocations	Being tacked, tackling, collisions with opponents
Running and endurance sports	Stress fractures, shin splints, runner's knee	Repetitive impact on joints, overtraining, improper footwear
Team sports (football, basketball)	Ankle sprains, knee injuries, ACL tears, strains	Abrupt stops and turns, collisions with opponents
Racket sports (tennis, badminton)	Tennis elbow, shoulder injuries, sprains	Repetitive arm movements, poor technique, intense rallies
Combat sports (boxing, MMA)	Cuts, bruises, fractures, concussions, dislocations	Punches, kicks, throws, direct impact with opponent
Gymnastics and acrobatics	Sprains, fractures, ligament tears, overuse injuries	Landing, falls, extreme body positions
Winter sports (skiing, snowboarding)	Fractures, sprains, strains, concussions	Collision with obstacles, falls on icy surfaces
Water sports (swimming, surfing)	Shoulder injuries, sprains, strains, concussion	Diving accidents, overuse of shoulder in swimming, wipeouts in surfing
Cycling	Knee pain, lower back pain	Prolonged sitting, repetitive pedalling motion, poor bike setup / fit

Draw lines to connect the injury with the corresponding sporting activity in which it commonly occurs. [4]

Common injury	Sporting situation
Concussion	Landing poorly in basketball
Ankle sprains	Repeated serves in tennis
Stress fractures	Punched in the head when boxing
Tennis elbow	Regular ground impact in running
	Poor body position in swimming

Concussion – Boxing,[1] **Ankle sprains** – Basketball,[1] **Stress fractures** – Running,[1] **Tennis elbow** – Tennis.[1]

1.1.2

COACHING, INSTRUCTING AND LEADING

Coaching is essential for shaping athlete performance, combining skill development, strategic planning, proper technique and injury prevention measures. Well-structured programs enhance abilities and reduce risk.

Knowledge of techniques, rules and regulations

Coaches with a high understanding of **techniques**, **rules** and **regulations** can guide performers effectively, minimising injury risks. For instance, a football coach with an in-depth knowledge of the rules can prevent players from engaging in dangerous play, reducing the likelihood of serious injuries such as fractures or concussion (**pages 34–35**).

> ⚠️ A coach lacking comprehensive knowledge may inadvertently encourage rule violation or improper techniques, leading to increased injury risks. A basketball coach unaware of proper shooting technique could potentially cause chronic shoulder strain (see **page 36**). A poorly informed boxing coach may teach that it is legal to hit below the belt.

Experience

Experienced coaches bring a wealth of insight, recognising potential hazards and employing effective training methods. A seasoned gymnastics coach, for instance, can guide athletes to perform complex routines safely, minimising the risk of injuries.

> ⚠️ Novice coaches, with few or no official coaching badges, may struggle to perform a proper risk assessment, increasing the likelihood of injuries. In weightlifting, an inexperienced coach may fail to recognise poor lifting form, contributing to acute injuries **page 29**.

Communication

Coaches with **strong communication skills** foster understanding and cooperation, ensuring performers quickly understand instructions and safety protocols. Effective communication can **prevent misunderstanding** of explanations, tactics and drills, reducing the risk of collisions and subsequent injuries.

> ⚠️ Poor communication may lead to confusion, with athletes unsure of instructions or safety guidelines. In a team sport, such as rugby, unclear communication from the coach may result in players executing plays improperly, increasing the risk of concussion (**page 35**) or fractures (**page 34**).

Supervision

Careful **supervision** by coaches during training sessions ensures everyone follows proper techniques and adheres to safety guidelines. In a swimming context, proper supervision can **prevent accidents** including drowning, and head injuries (**page 36**) from diving errors.

⚠️ Inadequate supervision may result in performers engaging in risky behaviours. For example, a lack of supervision during a trampolining or weightlifting session could lead to unsafe use of equipment, increasing the risk of injury.

Ethical standards and behaviour

Coaches with **high ethical standards** prioritise performer safety and well-being, and they **discourage dangerous practices** and **promote fair play**. In boxing, a coach with strong ethical behaviour ensures athletes engage in controlled, safe sparring in training to avoid serious injuries.

⚠️ An unethical sports coach may encourage players to play on with an injury, or promote the use of performance enhancing drugs which would contribute to longer term health issues, including cardiovascular problems.

Explain how an inexperienced trampoline coach could increase the risk of injury during a trampoline routine. Provide specific examples to highlight the potential impact. [2]

A coach may fail to provide proper technical guidance, increasing the risk of injuries.[1] For example, they may not teach landing techniques properly, leading to an awkward movement.[1] / They may not consider the individual's abilities and limitations, pushing them beyond their capability.[1] An example could be asking them to attempt a double forward somersault, leading to an awkward landing and injury.[1]

OCR Cambridge Nationals **Sport Science – R180: Topic Area 1**

1.1.3

ENVIRONMENT

The sporting environment greatly impacts performer safety. Properly maintained facilities, playing surfaces and weather considerations are essential for injury prevention. Neglecting these environmental factors increases risk.

Weather and temperature conditions

Excessive heat can lead to heat-related illnesses, such as heat exhaustion (**page 66**) or dehydration (**page 68**). Athletes, for example marathon runners, performing in hot conditions may experience severe consequences without proper hydration and cooling.

Cold temperatures increase the risk of hypothermia, particularly for winter sports athletes without proper clothing and protection. (See **page 64**.)

Fog reduces visibility which could cause collisions with other players, goal posts or holes in the playing surface.

Rain or **wet playing surfaces** can increase the likelihood of slipping, causing accidents and injuries, for example a twisted ankle, strain or sprain.

Playing surface (natural and artificial) and surrounding area

Uneven natural surfaces and terrain in sports (e.g. cross-country running) can result in ankle injuries. Hard artificial surfaces, such as Astro pitches or indoor courts should be checked for cracks or holes. They may also contribute to impact-related injuries, including abrasions, concussions and dislocations from slips and falls (see **pages 32–35**). Considerations in the surrounding area include corner flags, fencing and goal posts. Natural environments need to be checked for hazards such as litter, glass, wet leaves and animal waste. A skiing piste needs to be checked for rocks, tree stumps and ice.

Different playing surfaces can affect the choice and performance of footwear, for example, running spikes for the track, clay and grass court tennis shoes. See **pages 8-9**.

Weather conditions and playing surfaces play crucial roles in sports safety.

Provide **one** example of how weather conditions can influence the type of playing surface chosen and explain how this may contribute to injury prevention. [3]

Heavy rainfall may soften natural grass on a playing field and create a water-logged pitch.[1] Therefore, playing on a well-drained artificial pitch can prevent waterlogging,[1] reducing the risk of slips and falls.[1] / Snow and freezing temperatures can affect outdoor playing surfaces.[1] Choosing to play on an indoor court in the winter months,[1] prevents injuries and medical conditions associated with cold and icy temperatures.[1]

Human interaction

Other performers

In contact sports, such as boxing and rugby, intense physical interactions between performers can lead to injuries. Powerful **punches in boxing** or high impact **collisions** during tackles in rugby pose significant injury risk. In non-contact sports that require communication between performers, like doubles tennis or synchronised diving, **miscommunication** or mistimed movements between performers may result in injuries. In association football, **shirt-pulling** and **pushing** can also lead to **aggressive acts** that might cause **injury**.

Officials

Sports referees or officials can be accidentally **hit by balls** or players during fast-paced gameplay, leading to injury. Officials also have a responsibility to punish dangerous fouls (e.g. a two-footed tackle in football) and aggressive behaviour in order to maintain a safe environment.

Spectators

In instances of crowd disturbances during events such as football matches, spectators may suffer injuries through **crushing**. **Hooliganism** or **stray objects**, such as golf balls, can also pose a risk.

1.1.4

EQUIPMENT

Many sports use specific equipment to improve performance and reduce the risk or severity of injury. However, equipment that is poorly fitted, incorrectly used or not looked after properly, can lead to injury.

Protective equipment

Protective equipment is designed to safeguard athletes from direct impact and potential injury during sporting activity. Examples include helmets, shin pads, mouthguards, and goggles. When used correctly, protective equipment can significantly reduce the risk of severe injuries.

Example: Helmets in non-contact sports, for example, cricket, cycling and skiing, provide crucial head protection. However, improperly fitted or neglected head gear can lead to head injuries, fractures, or facial trauma (see **pages 34–35**).

Performance equipment

Performance equipment aims to enhance an athlete's abilities, often including items such as specialised rackets, bats, or technical gear. Well-designed performance equipment can contribute to improved skill execution and efficiency, reducing the risk of certain injuries.

Example: Using the right type of tennis racket can minimise the strain on an athlete's arm. However, using equipment that is incompatible with an individual's skill level or not properly maintained, may lead to muscle strains or overuse injuries. (See **pages 31 and 36**) Being hit by performance equipment, such as a cricket ball, could cause a fracture of the arm.

Helmets are an example of protective equipment in sports that aim to reduce the risk and severity of injury.

State **one** other example of protective equipment and explain how it contributes to injury prevention. [2]

Examples include: Knee pads[1] provide cushioning and support for the knee joints, reducing the impact force during falls or collisions.[1] / Mouthguards[1] act as a barrier, absorbing impact forces during contact sports.[1] / Shin guards[1] provide a shield for the lower leg, reducing the risk of bruising and fractures of the lower leg.[1] Hard-wearing leather rugby boots[1] can prevent a fracture in the foot if it gets stamped on[1] in a ruck.

Clothing

Clothing in sports serves various purposes, from regulating body temperature to providing comfort and flexibility.

Example: Compression garments can aid muscle support. However, wearing clothing that hinders movement or lacks appropriate ventilation may contribute to overheating, dehydration (**page 68**), skin rashes or muscle cramp.

Footwear

Footwear is a critical aspect of sports equipment, impacting an athlete's performance and injury risk. Properly fitting and sport specific shoes provide support, stability, and shock absorption.

Example: Using running shoes with inadequate arch supports may lead to shin splints or stress fractures (**page 40**). Poorly fitting footwear or a lack of grip (e.g. incorrectly using studs on Astroturf or trainers on grass) can result in slips, falls and ankle injuries.

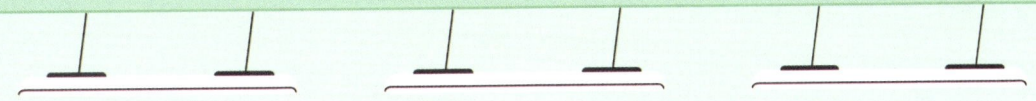

1.2.1

INTRINSIC FACTORS

Intrinsic risk factors originate from within an individual performer. These characteristics are collectively referred to as **individual variables**. They each influence both the risk and severity of injury.

The extrinsic (outside) factors are on **page 2**.

Individual variables

Gender

Gender can significantly affect the risk of injury in sports due to inherent biological and physiological differences between males and females. Differences in muscle mass, strength and body composition between genders can influence how forces are absorbed and transmitted through the body during sports activities.

Age

As individuals **age**, physiological changes in muscle strength, flexibility and bone density affect how the body responds to the physical demands of sporting activity. For instance, older individuals may experience a decline in muscle mass and flexibility, impacting their ability to absorb shock and maintain joint stability during sports.

Experience

Experience relates to an athlete's exposure to the demands of their chosen activity. Novice athletes, regardless of age, often face a higher risk of injuries due to their unfamiliarity with proper techniques, movement patterns and the overall dynamics of their sport. As athletes gain experience, they develop a better understanding of how to pace themselves, execute skills and make decisions.

Weight

Body weight can affect how forces are distributed throughout the musculoskeletal system during sporting activity. Individuals with higher body weight may experience increased stress on joints, potentially increasing the risk of injuries such as knee or ankle sprains (**page 31**), or stress fractures (**page 40**). On the other hand, athletes with lower body weight may be more susceptible to injuries related to inadequate shock absorption. Engaging in high-intensity exercise can elevate heart rate significantly which may pose challenges for individuals with higher BMI, owing to added strain on the cardiovascular system.

Fitness levels

Athletes with high **fitness levels** are better equipped to meet the demands of their sport while minimising the risk of injury. Well-conditioned athletes typically demonstrate enhanced endurance, strength, and flexibility. Whereas, individuals with lower fitness levels may experience quicker fatigue, reduced muscular support and reduced coordination, increasing their risk exposure to injury.

Technique and ability

Technique and **ability** directly impact how athletes move and respond to the demands of their chosen activity. Proficient technique ensures optimal precision in skill execution, reducing the likelihood of injury. A high level of ability empowers athletes to make informed decisions, react effectively and execute complex movements with precision, contributing to a safer and more effective sports performance. Poor technique can cause chronic health issues.

Nutrition and hydration

Adequate **nutrition** provides the essential proteins, vitamins and minerals needed for energy production, muscle function and recovery, reducing the risk of fatigue-related injuries. **Hydration** regulates body temperature and supports physiological functions during exercise, minimising the risk of dehydration related issues (**page 68**) including loss of focus and concentration.

Medical conditions

Pre-existing **medical conditions** such as joint disorders, cardiovascular issues or respiratory illness may require special consideration in training and competition to minimise associated risks. Some medications used to manage medical conditions can impact levels of hydration, endurance and heat tolerance, further increasing the risk of injury.

Sleep

Sleep directly affects physical and cognitive function. Inadequate or disrupted sleep patterns can lead to fatigue, impaired reaction times and poor decision making, increasing the risk of injury. A good quality of sleep is essential for the body's recovery processes, including tissue repair and the release of growth hormones, contributing to overall physical well-being.

Previous and recurring injuries

Athletes who have suffered an injury will be at an increased risk of suffering the same injury again. Targeted rehabilitation and preventative measures, such as strapping or taping, help to reduce the risk of recurring problems.

Individual variables can also be connected. For example, how much someone weighs can affect how fit they are. This shows that an athlete's situation is complex, and it is important to customise training and injury prevention to make sure they perform well and stay healthy.

Compare and contrast how different intrinsic factors can influence the risk and severity of injury. [3]

Examples include: Age: Both younger and older individuals may be more susceptible to certain injuries due to developmental factors.[1] Younger individuals might face risks related to growth plate injuries,[1] while older individuals may experience injuries associated with aging, such as joint degeneration.[1] / Fitness levels: Both highly trained athletes and unfit people can face injury risks.[1] Unfit individuals may be prone to injuries due to a weaker musculoskeletal system,[1] while athletes may face overuse injuries from intense training.[1]

OCR Cambridge Nationals **Sport Science – R180: Topic Area 1**

PSYCHOLOGICAL FACTORS

Four main psychological factors contribute towards the risk of injury in sport.

Motivation

Motivation is the internal or external drive that directs behaviour towards a goal.

Scenario A: In a crucial cup match, a player is **highly motivated** to win and showcase their skills. The player may exhibit risk-taking behaviour, attempting aggressive tackles or pushing themselves beyond their physical limits to contribute to the team's success. Potential injuries could be strains and sprains (**page 31**).

> Aggression is also a psychological factor when dealing with sports injuries. See **page 14**.

Scenario B: In a mid-season friendly match of little significance, a player has **low motivation**. The player may lack focus and put minimal effort into preparation, leading to decreased awareness and engagement on the field. This may increase the risk of injuries due to a lack of focus, e.g. getting caught off guard, or potential muscle injuries owing to an inadequate warm up.

Arousal

Arousal is the level of physiological and psychological activation and readiness.

Scenario C: In the final minutes of a championship match, a rugby player experiences intense excitement and **arousal**. Fuelled by this, the player engages in overly aggressive tackles, increasing the risk of injuring themselves and their opponents. This may lead to concussion (**page 35**) or head injuries from forceful tackles, as well as fractures (**page 34**) due to the intensified physicality on the pitch.

Scenario D: In a less critical, early-season match with a significant point lead, a rugby player experiences **low arousal** levels. With reduced physiological and psychological activation, the player may lack the necessary focus and intensity, potentially leading to mistimed tackles and poor decision making on the field. The decreased arousal state increases susceptibility to injuries, for example, dislocations (**page 34**) after forceful impact with the ground.

Anxiety and stress

Anxiety is a negative emotional state that is characterised by apprehension and fear. Stress is the body's response to cope with the demands placed on us.

Scenario E: In a high-stakes netball game, a player experiences **high anxiety and stress** owing to the intense pressure to secure victory. Heightened anxiety and stress levels lead to increased muscle tension, impaired decision making and decreased coordination. These effects elevate the risk of injury such as a twisted ankle, resulting from mistimed movements or sudden changes in direction.

Confidence

Confidence is the belief in one's own ability to successfully complete a task.

Scenario F: In a crucial tournament final, a table tennis player enters with **high levels of confidence**, having performed exceptionally well in the preceding matches. The heightened confidence translates into assertive and aggressive play, enhancing overall performance. However, the increased assertiveness also elevates the risk of injuries during the match. A potential injury could be a muscle strain (**page 31**) resulting from more powerful strokes and quick movements.

Scenario G: After a series of losses, a table tennis player enters a match with **low confidence**, impacting their assertiveness and overall game approach. Their hesitancy and lack of assertiveness increases their vulnerability to injury. Mistimed movement across the table could potentially cause a trip, falling on the corner of the table and resulting in a cut or graze (**page 32**).

Complete the table to show how each psychological factor could increase the risk of injury. [3]

Psychological factor	Impact on injury risk
High confidence	(a)
Low arousal	(b)
Elevated aggression	(c)

Answers may include: (a) Positive influence on performance while minimising severe injuries.[1] (b) Increased susceptibility to injury through mistimed movements or collisions.[1] (c) Higher risk injuries related to overexertion and more intense play.[1]

1.2.2–1.2.3

AGGRESSION

Aggression in sport can be expressed through physical and non-physical means, with or without the intent to cause harm.

Performers must ensure that any acts of aggression are within the rules of their sport.

Direct aggression

Direct aggression is to engage in behaviours with the intent to cause harm or gain advantage through physical contact.

Example: In a heated rivalry match, an ice hockey player displays **direct aggression** by engaging in overly physical and confrontational plays. This (direct) aggression significantly increases the risk of injuries, including fractures (**page 34**), contusions (**page 32**) and head injuries (**page 35**). Deliberate actions aimed at opponents, including powerful body checks or collisions, contribute to a heightened physical intensity, elevating the potential severity of injuries.

Acts of non-contact aggression include smashing a shuttlecock hard during a rally, throwing a helmet on the ground, shouting at an umpire or deliberately breaking a tennis racket.

Channelled aggression

Channelled aggression requires redirecting aggressive energy towards increasing your performance without causing harm.

Example: In a disciplined and strategic playoff game, the ice hockey player channels aggression positively by focusing on assertive but controlled plays within the rules. Channelled aggression contributes to enhanced performance without compromising sportsmanship. Potential injuries are limited to minor incidents such as bruises or strains resulting from intense but regulated physical play.

---

1. Figure 1 shows a rugby tackle during an England v Scotland match at the 2023 Guinness 6 Nations match at Twickenham.

   Using Figure 1, explain **one** type of aggression shown in the behaviour of the players. [2]

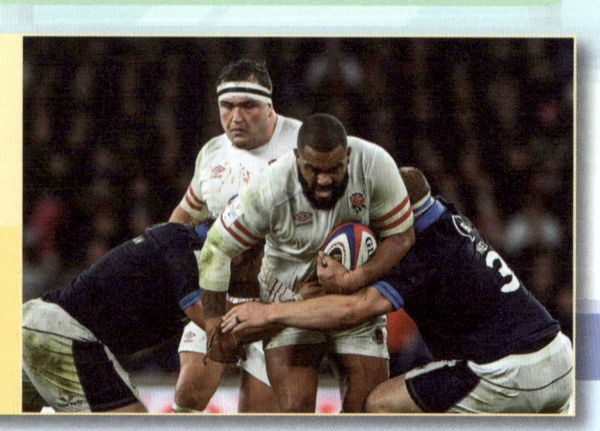

   1. Direct aggression[1] because they are making deliberate physical contact with each other with the intent to gain advantage.[1] / Channelled aggression[1] through assertive tackles / play without the intention of causing harm.[1]

Reasons for aggression

Level of performance

Aggression arising from the desire to outperform opponents or meet personal performance standards.

In a high-stakes basketball match, a player, driven by their desire to excel, engages in aggressive plays with more intense attack and defence to improve their team's performance.

Retaliation

Aggression as a response to perceived provocation, often a physical or verbal act from an opponent.

In a football match, a player retaliates aggressively after receiving a harsh tackle from an opponent, responding with a strong challenge or confrontation.

Retaliation is the act of responding to an action or situation with a counteraction.

Pressure to win

Aggression fuelled by external expectations and the intense desire to win, originating from **performers**, **coaches** or **spectators**.

In a championship tennis match, a player feels immense pressure from their coach, teammates, and a passionate crowd. The pressure to win contributes to aggressive shot-making and emotional outbursts on the court.

Decisions of officials

Aggression triggered by perceived unfair or incorrect decisions made by sports officials, leading to frustration and aggressive behaviour.

In a netball game, a team reacts aggressively when an umpire makes a controversial call, leading players to express dissatisfaction through aggressive protest or confrontations.

Use of performance enhancing drugs

Aggression can be influenced by the use of substances that enhance physical abilities.

A rider in a cycling competition, under the influence of performance enhancing drugs, uses aggressive language, gestures and tactics, including risky manoeuvres and overly assertive positioning in the peloton.

---

2. In the 2006 World Cup Final, Zinedine Zidane acted aggressively by headbutting Marco Materazzi in response to verbal provocation. State **one** reason for this aggression. [1]

2. Retaliation / pressure to win. [1]

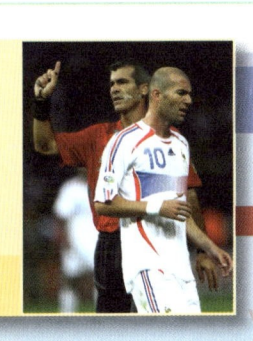

OCR Cambridge Nationals **Sport Science – R180: Topic Area 1**

1.2.4

MENTAL STRATEGIES

Mental strategies are tools used to enhance performance and manage stress. They help improve an athlete's mental resilience and can significantly impact their success.

Mental rehearsal

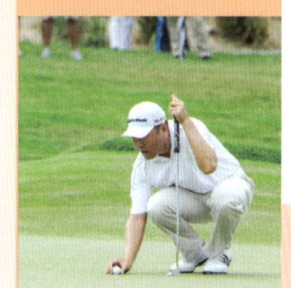

Mental rehearsal, also known as **mental practice** or **visualisation**, involves imagining positive outcomes, visualising specific skills, actions or performances without physical movements. It is often used as part of an effective **warm up** (**see page 18**). Benefits include skill enhancement by refining and reinforcing motor skills, performance preparation by mentally preparing for competition, and anxiety reduction by remaining calm and focusing on the performance.

Example: A golfer mentally rehearses each swing, visualising the perfect form and trajectory of the ball, before taking the shot.

Imagery

Imagery involves creating vivid mental images or sensations related to a desired performance or positive outcome. Benefits include increased confidence and self-belief, and stress management through positive mental images. It can also improve an athlete's focus by enhancing concentration and mental simulation of successful actions.

Example: A gymnast envisions himself performing a flawless routine, feeling the movements, hearing the applause, and seeing himself land successfully.

Selective attention

Selective attention is the ability to focus on relevant cues while ignoring irrelevant distractions. Benefits include improved concentration on specific elements crucial for optimal performance, improved decision making by filtering out distractions, and increased consistency by maintaining focus for a more stable performance.

Example: A tennis player, during a crucial tiebreaker in a grand slam final, strategically focuses attention on the opponent's serving patterns and body language while selectively blocking out crowd noise and distractions.

Greg Rutherford, a former British long jumper and Olympic gold medallist, used imagery as part of his metal preparation for the long jump.

Define imagery and explain how it may have benefited Greg's performance in the long jump. [3]

Imagery is a mental strategy in which an individual creates vivid mental images related to a desired performance.[1] Imagery could have contributed to enhancing his confidence[1] by allowing him to mentally visualise a successful jump.[1] / Imagery could have played a role in refining his technique[1] by mentally rehearsing each phase of the jump.[1]

Topic Area 1

EXAMINATION PRACTICE

Topic area 1: Different factors which influence the risk and severity of injury

1. Which **one** of the following intrinsic psychological factors is most closely associated with an athlete's internal drive towards a goal? [1]
   - ☐ A – Anxiety
   - ☐ B – Arousal
   - ☐ C – Confidence
   - ☐ D – Motivation

2. Sleep is an individual variable that can influence injury risk and severity in sport.
   (a) State **three** other individual variables. [3]
   (b) Describe the potential impact of insufficient sleep on the likelihood of injuries in athletes. [2]

3. Other than weather, identify **two** environmental factors that can influence injury when playing sport. [2]

4. Complete the table below by filling in the blanks with the appropriate mental strategy type or description. [3]

Mental Strategy	Description
(a)	Refining and reinforcing motor skills
Imagery	(b)
(c)	Enhancing concentration and mental simulation

5. Explain the significance of proper technique and instruction in coaching for injury prevention. [2]

6. Explain how high levels of anxiety can impact an athlete's performance and injury risk during a competitive sports event. [2]

7. Explain how pressure to win from performers, coaches and spectators can contribute to aggression in sport. Provide a sporting example. [3]

8. Many sports use equipment that aims to improve performance and reduce the risk and severity of injury if used properly. However, the same equipment can potentially lead to injury.

   Evaluate the significance of different types of equipment in ensuring athlete safety during sporting activity. [8]

OCR Cambridge Nationals **Sport Science – R180: Topic Area 1**

2.1

KEY COMPONENTS OF A WARM UP

A warm up is a simple exercise routine that prepares the body for more intense physical activity. Warm ups will vary from person to person, and from one activity to another. However, there are four key components of a warm up:

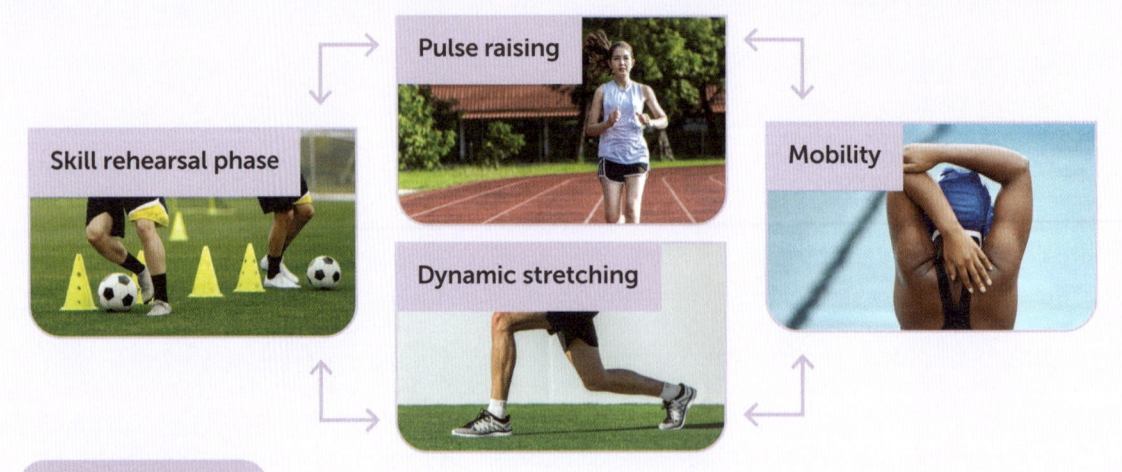

- Skill rehearsal phase
- Pulse raising
- Dynamic stretching
- Mobility

Pulse raising

Pulse raising gradually increases the heart rate to **increase blood flow** and **oxygen** to the **working muscles**. This prepares them for a game or more intense activity. It typically involves low to moderate intensity aerobic exercise, typically lasting 5 to 10 minutes.

Light jogging
Start with a slow jog, for example, around a football pitch, and gradually increase the pace to elevate the heart rate. The same process could be used if swimming or cycling.

Skipping
This is an effective way to raise the heart rate while engaging the muscles in the lower body. Boxers are well known for their ability to skip as it is a common pulse raiser in boxing.

Mobility

The **mobility** phase focuses on enhancing joint **flexibility**, **range of motion**, and overall mobility. This part of the warm up is crucial for **reducing the risk of injury** and improving the efficiency of movements during more intense activities.

Arm circles
Rotate your arms in a circular motion, both clockwise and anticlockwise to warm the shoulder joints. This could be used by swimmers before the 50m Butterfly event.

Leg swings
Stand near a support, such as a wall, and swing one leg forwards and backwards or side to side, promoting flexibility at the hip joint.

Dynamic stretching

Dynamic stretching is an extension of the mobility phase involving **stretching whilst moving** to lengthen or increase the **flexibility** of the muscles. Exercises should be linked to similar movements related to the main activity.

High knees

March in place while lifting your knees as high as comfortable, engaging the muscles at the hips.

Walking lunges

Take a step forward and lower your body by bending both knees until the back knee nearly touches the ground with the front knee being at a 90-degree angle. Repeat on the opposite leg. Volleyball players may use lunges as they improve power in the legs to quickly change direction before accelerating and decelerating.

Skill rehearsal phase

The **skill rehearsal phase** is designed to prepare the athlete mentally and physically for the specific movements or skills they will be performing during the main activity. It should use common movement patterns related to the sport, such as set pieces and drills.

Drills and repetition

Specific drills, such as dribbling or passing, that mimic the key movements of the main activity can be repeated. A Basketball player may practice free throw shots as part of their skills rehearsal.

Sport specific movements

A movement could be performed that closely resembles those required in the main activity. A footballer might practice pivoting for changes in direction or a badminton player may practice serves.

Complete the table below, outlining **one** example for each phase of a sports warm up specific to a goalkeeper in football. [4]

Warm up phase	Example exercise
Pulse raising	(a)
Mobility	(b)
Dynamic stretching	(c)
Skill rehearsal phase	(d)

Answers may include: (a) Pulse raising – Light jogging around the penalty area / pitch.[1]
(b) Mobility – Arm circles / leg swings.[1] (c) Dynamic stretching – Quick footwork drills / walking lunges.[1] (d) Skill rehearsal phase – Practicing goal kicks / throws.[1]

2.2.1

PHYSIOLOGICAL BENEFITS OF A WARM UP

Warming up significantly increases an athlete's ability to train to a higher level, to train more frequently, to avoid injury and to achieve better results. A warm up before physical activity offers several physiological benefits. These include:

Physiological benefits to the cardio-respiratory system

Increase in heart rate

As the muscles engage in physical activity throughout the warm up phases, they demand more oxygen. To meet this increased demand, the **cardio-respiratory system** (heart and lungs) works harder, delivering more **oxygenated blood to the working muscles**.

Physiological benefits to the musculoskeletal system

Increase in muscle temperature

Warm muscles contract and relax more efficiently than cold ones. An increase in **muscle temperature** improves flexibility and reduces the risk of muscle strains and injuries.

Increase in flexibility of muscles and joints

A warm up includes **dynamic stretching**, which helps improve joint flexibility and range of motion throughout the **musculoskeletal system**. This can contribute to better performance and reduce the risk of injury, especially in activities that involve rapid movements.

Increase in pliability of ligaments and tendons

Warming up increases the **suppleness** of connective tissues and reduces muscle stiffness. This is particularly important for activities that involve repetitive or intense movements.

Increase in blood flow and oxygen to muscles

A warm up gradually increases your heart rate, leading to an increase in blood flow to the muscles. This helps deliver oxygen and nutrients to the working muscles, preparing them for the upcoming activity.

Increase in the speed of muscle contraction

A warm up stimulates the nervous system, promoting faster and more efficient communication between the brain and muscles. This can enhance coordination and reaction time during physical activity.

1. Which **one** of the following is **not** a physiological benefit of a warm up? [1]
   A - Increased blood flow
   B - Increased concentration
   C - Increased flexibility
   D - Increased temperature
2. Explain how a warm-up contributes to the reduction of muscle stiffness. [2]
3. Describe **one** way in which warming up prepares the cardiovascular system for physical activity. [2]

1. B: Increased concentration.[1]

2. A warm-up increases the suppleness of connective tissues,[1] making them more flexible.[1] / A warm-up increases the temperature of muscles,[1] making them more pliable.[1]

3. Gradually increasing heart rate,[1] ensuring that the heart is ready to meet the increased demands of physical activity.[1] / Increased blood flow,[1] allows more oxygen to be delivered to the working muscles to meet the demands of physical activity.[1]

Suppleness refers to how flexible and pliable something is. Pliable muscles are long, soft and strong.

2.2.2

PSYCHOLOGICAL BENEFITS OF A WARM UP

While warm ups are primarily associated with physiological benefits, they also have psychological advantages that contribute to an overall improved mental state and readiness for physical activity. Some of those psychological benefits include:

Heighten or control arousal levels

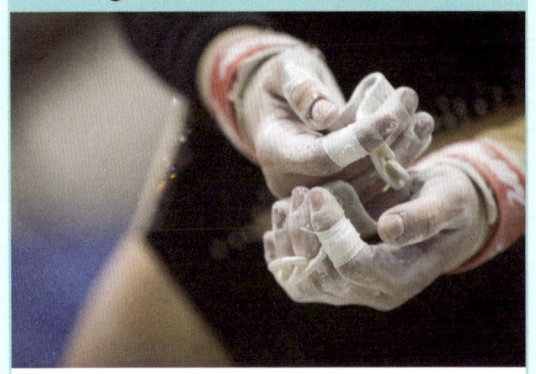

This is also known as 'getting in the zone'. A warm up can create a positive state of arousal, increasing alertness and mental readiness. For others, a warm up can serve as a tool to manage anxiety associated with the physical activity ahead.

Improve concentration / focus

A warm up allows an individual to shift their focus from a resting state to an active and alert state. This transition can enhance concentration and mental readiness for the physical activity ahead.

Increase motivation

Participating in a warm up boosts motivation by signalling the start of physical activity, intensifying the drive to perform well, and encouraging greater effort.

Increase confidence

Completing a warm up can instil a sense of accomplishment and boost self-confidence. This positive mindset can carry over into the main physical activity, contributing to better performance.

Mental rehearsal

This is a cognitive technique where individuals mentally visualise and simulate the upcoming physical activity or performance. It involves creating a mental image of the actions, movements, and successful execution of the activity before engaging in it.

Negative effects if no warm-up is performed

Skipping a warm-up before engaging in physical activity can have several negative effects on the body. Potential consequences of not warming up include:

Increased risk of injury → Reduced joint flexibility → Poor performance → Delayed muscle response → Increased muscle soreness ↓

Mental unpreparedness ← Increased lactic acid build up ← Limited blood flow to muscles ← Stress on heart ← Impaired oxygen delivery

---

Describe how a warm up contributes to a badminton player's focus and concentration during a match. [2]

It will shift their mental state from rest to an active / alert mode,[1] enhancing readiness for strategic and precise shots.[1]

OCR Cambridge Nationals **Sport Science – R180: Topic Area 2**

2.3 KEY COMPONENTS OF A COOL DOWN

A cool down is a set of exercises or activities performed after the main part of a physical activity and involves two key components: pulse lowering and stretching.

Pulse lowering

Pulse lowering focuses on gradually reducing the exercise intensity, to bring down the heart rate and breathing rate back towards its resting state. This phase typically lasts about five minutes.

Example:

Light aerobic exercise – activities like slow jogging, walking, or cycling at a gentle pace help to gradually decrease the heart rate.

Stretching

Maintenance stretches

Maintenance stretches are intended to maintain your range of motion with less emphasis on improvement. They help prevent muscle tightness and should be held for 10–15 seconds.

Examples:

Standing hamstring stretch – This can help maintain flexibility in the back of the thighs. Athletes whose sports involves lots of running, such as cross country, would benefit.

Shoulder cross-body stretch – This would be of benefit to an athlete competing in the javelin, for example, to maintain flexibility of the deltoids.

24 ClearRevise

Static stretching

Static stretches involve gradually elongating a muscle or muscle group to the point of mild discomfort in a fixed stretch position and holding this for a set duration, typically 15 to 60 seconds. This can be repeated two or three times.

Examples:

Lower back and glute stretch – A cyclist might use this stretch to prevent lower back pain and to improve overall comfort, flexibility, and long-term cycling performance.	**Hip flexor stretch** – A gymnast would use this stretch to improve flexibility, leg extension and splits to execute skills with better form and position.

Proprioceptive Neuromuscular Facilitation (PNF)

PNF is an advanced form of stretching that involves contracting a muscle during the stretch. It is often performed with a partner or immoveable object, and is known for its effectiveness in improving flexibility and range of motion. PNF stretching involves three main phases:

1. Passive stretch – a muscle or muscle group is stretched to its limits and held in that position without any effort from the person being stretched.
2. Isometric contraction – after reaching the passive stretch, the muscle is contracted against resistance (e.g. a wall, partner or stretching band) while it remains in the stretch position. This creates an **isometric muscle contraction**.
3. Passive stretch (again) – After the isometric contraction, the muscle is passively stretched again. This time, the muscle tends to relax more, allowing for a deeper stretch.

> An **isometric muscle contraction** maintains a static position and does not create movement. The muscle will not change length as the muscle force is equal to the resistance. The muscle contracts but does not change length.

Which **one** of the following types of stretches should **not** be completed as part of an effective cool down? [1]

A - Dynamic stretch

B - Maintenance stretch

C - PNF stretch

D - Static stretch

A: Dynamic stretch.[1] (Which raises muscle temperature rather than cooling it down gradually.)

2.4

PHYSIOLOGICAL BENEFITS OF A COOL DOWN

The primary purpose of a cool down is to gradually transition the body from the heightened state of activity back to a state of rest, aimed at promoting recovery. A cool down after physical activity offers several physiological benefits. These include:

Physiological benefits

Gradually lowers heart rate

During exercise, your heart rate will increase. A cool down helps to gradually lower your heart rate to its resting level. The gradual reduction is important for cardiovascular health and prevents abrupt changes that can strain the cardiovascular system.

Gradually lowers temperature

A cool down allows your body temperature to gradually return to its normal range. This helps prevent the abrupt cooling of muscles, reducing the risk of muscle cramps and stiffness.

Circulates blood and oxygen

A cool down ensures a gradual reduction in oxygen demand by the working muscles. This is important for maintaining a balance between oxygen supply and demand, preventing oxygen deprivation in tissues, and reducing the risk of light-headedness or fainting.

Helps prevent blood pooling

Intense exercise can cause blood vessels in muscles to dilate. A cool down with light aerobic activity helps prevent blood from pooling in the muscles, reducing the risk of muscle cramps and soreness.

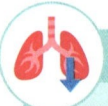

Gradually reduces breathing rate

A cool down will help the respiratory system transition from a state of exercise to a more relaxed state, preventing a sudden drop in oxygen levels that contributes to a smoother recovery process.

Removes waste products such as lactic acid

Exercise produces waste by-products such as lactic acid. A cool down aids in the gradual removal of these waste products by promoting circulation, which can help reduce muscle soreness and stiffness.

Reduces risk of Delayed Onset of Muscle Soreness (DOMS)

DOMS refers to the discomfort or pain that may be felt in muscles 24–72 hours after intense exercise. A cool down will help reduce DOMS by aiding in the removal of lactic acid and other waste products accumulated during intense physical activity.

Negative effects if no cool down is performed

Skipping a cool down after exercise can have several negative effects on the body. Some potential consequences of not cooling down include:

Blood pooling → Decreased oxygen delivery → Increased risk of injury → Delayed recovery

Elevated blood pressure ← Elevated heart rate ← Impaired flexibility ← Muscle stiffness and soreness

---

Explain the role of a cool down in preventing blood pooling in the muscles after intense exercise. [3]

During intense exercise, the blood vessels in the working muscles dilate to meet the demands of oxygen.[1] Completing a cool down, instead of an abrupt stop, will sustain blood circulation,[1] ensuring that the blood continues to flow from the muscles back to the heart.[1] Gradually reducing exercise intensity during a cool down helps bring the body back to a resting state,[1] thereby preventing blood from pooling in the muscles.

When talking about a cool down, you should emphasise a gradual effect, rather than to just lower heart rate.

Topic Area 2

EXAMINATION PRACTICE

Topic area 2: Warm up and cool down routines

1. Which **one** of the following is **not** a key component of a warmup? [1]
   - ☐ A – Dynamic stretching
   - ☐ B – Mobility
   - ☐ C – Pulse raising
   - ☐ D – Static stretching

2. Which **one** of the following activities could be used as a pulse raiser? [1]
   - ☐ A – Deep breathing
   - ☐ B – Light jog
   - ☐ C – Meditation
   - ☐ D – PNF stretches

3. Hannah plays hockey. Before competing in a hockey match, she undertakes an extensive warm-up so that she is physiologically prepared.

   (a) State **three** physiological effects of warming up and explain a different benefit for each. [6]

Effect 1:	Benefit 1:
Effect 2:	Benefit 2:
Effect 3:	Benefit 3:

   (b) After the hockey match, Hannah completes a cool down.
   State **three** benefits of cooling down immediately after exercise. [3]

   (c) Complete the table below, outlining the **two** phases of the cool down and **one** example exercise for each, specific to hockey. [4]

Cool down phase	Example exercise
(i)	(ii)
(iii)	(iv)

28 ClearRevise

3.1.1

ACUTE INJURIES

Acute injuries are sudden and immediate injuries that occur because of a specific **trauma** or incident. These injuries typically happen suddenly, are often unforeseen, and can range from mild to severe.

Acute injuries are intricately linked with both extrinsic (1.1) and intrinsic (1.2) factors. Extrinsic factors, such as the type of activity, the quality of coaching, the environment and the equipment can significantly contribute to the likelihood and severity of acute injuries. Simultaneously, intrinsic factors and individual variables play a crucial role in determining their susceptibility to such injuries.

Sudden trauma

Sudden trauma refers to a forceful and unexpected event or injury that occurs abruptly, often resulting in immediate damage or harm to the body. This type of trauma is characterised by its rapid onset, and it can be caused by various incidents such as falls, collisions, impacts, or other accidents.

Immediate impact and pain

Immediate impact and pain are fundamental aspects of acute injuries resulting from sudden trauma. When an injury occurs, the body experiences a rapid and forceful interaction with an external force, leading to an immediate impact on the affected area. At the same time, the body's nervous system responds to the trauma by transmitting signals of pain to the brain. Pain serves as a protective response, signalling the presence of damage.

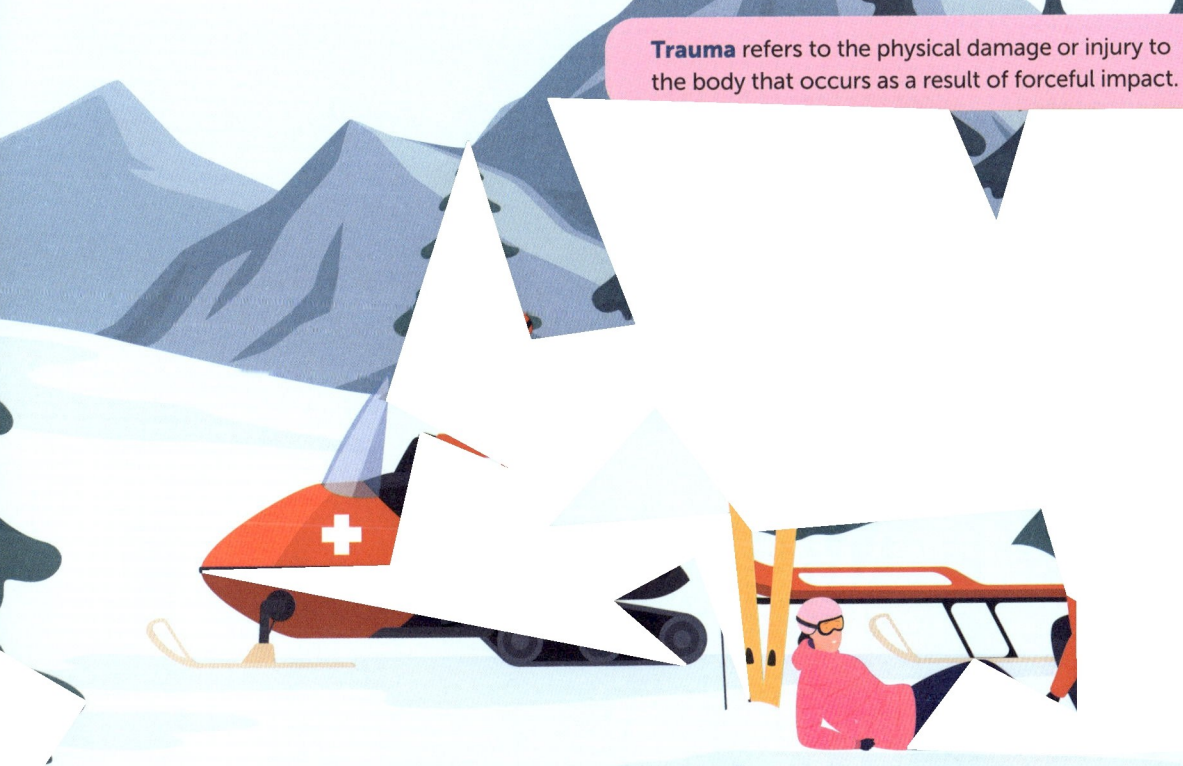

Trauma refers to the physical damage or injury to the body that occurs as a result of forceful impact.

3.1.2

SOFT TISSUE AND HARD TISSUE INJURIES

Soft tissue injuries

Soft tissue injuries are common acute sporting injuries that include a range of trauma to muscles, tendons and ligaments, impacting how the body moves and is supported. Ways to reduce the risk of soft tissue injuries are to complete a thorough warm up, to use proper techniques and to make gradual rather than rapid progression.

Example: In table tennis, a player is engaged in a fast-paced rally. As the opponent delivers a strong and unexpected shot to the side of the table, the player quickly moves laterally to reach the ball. In the process, the player overexerts the muscles involved, leading to a soft tissue injury, such as a groin strain.

Hard tissue injuries

Hard tissue injuries are common acute sporting injures involving trauma to the skeletal structure that provides the body's framework. These injuries predominately consist of fractures and dislocations, where the bones bear the brunt of forceful impacts or awkward landings. Ways to reduce the risk of hard tissue injuries are to wear protective gear, and use proper form and technique.

Example: In football, two players are competing for a high ball in the air. As they both jump to make a header, there's a collision between their heads. The force of the impact may lead to a hard tissue injury, such as a facial fracture or a broken nose.

Injury	Causes	Symptoms	Treatment (See Topic Area 4)
Soft tissue	Impact, overstretching, sudden movements	Pain, swelling, bruising	Protection, rest, ice, compression, elevation, pain relief
Hard tissue	Impact, direct force	Pain, swelling, deformity	Immobilisation, medical assessment, possible surgery

3.1.3–3.1.4

STRAINS AND SPRAINS

Strains

Strains involve overstretched or **torn muscles or tendons**. These injuries often arise from abrupt movements, forceful impacts, or inadequate warm-up, placing strain on the fibres that enable muscle and tendon function. Muscles that are common to strains in sport are the hamstrings, quadriceps and back muscles. The Achilles tendon at the ankle is also prone to strain.

> **Tendons** connect muscles to bones, allowing for movement and stability in the joints.

Example: In athletics, a sprinter in the 100m exerts an intense force during the initial acceleration phase. Due to the rapid and powerful push-off from the starting blocks, the muscles involved are subject to significant stress. If the athlete has not warmed up properly, the muscles may be prone to overstretching or tearing, leading to a strain.

Injury	Causes	Symptoms	Treatment (See Topic Area 4)
Torn muscle or tendon	Sudden force, overuse	Sharp pain, weakness, swelling	Rest, ice, compression, elevation, physical therapy, possible surgery

Sprains

Sprains involve overstretched or **torn ligaments**, often the consequence of sudden twists, impacts, or awkward landing during physical activity. The ankle, knee and wrist joints are common sites of sprains in sport. Ways of reducing the risk of sprains in sport are to complete strengthening exercises, execute proper technique and balance training.

> **Ligaments** connect bones to bones and provide joint stability.
>
> The **ACL** is one of the major ligaments in the knee.

Example: In a trampoline routine, a trampolinist is performing a series of somersaults. If they lose control, misjudge the landing, or under rotate, leading to an awkward landing with force applied to the ankle, the impact and twisting motion upon landing can result in overstretching or tearing the ligaments around the ankle, causing a sprain.

Injury	Causes	Symptoms	Treatment (See Topic Area 4)
Torn ligaments, e.g. **Anterior Cruciate Ligament (ACL)**	Sudden twisting or impact	Severe pain, swelling, instability	PRICE, bracing, physical therapy, surgery

---

During a school netball match, a player suddenly feels a sharp pain in the back of their calf muscle while sprinting to intercept a ball. The player limps off the court and is unable to continue playing.

Describe **one** preventative measure that the player could have taken to reduce the risk of the strain. [2]

A proper warm up,[1] increasing the temperature in the muscles would make them more pliable[1]. / Strength training,[1] would build muscle resilience in the calf muscles.[1] / Static stretching,[1] would enhance the flexibility of the calf muscles.[1]

3.1.5

SKIN DAMAGE

Engaging in sports and physical activities involves contact of the skin with various surfaces, individuals, and equipment. Such interactions can result in skin damage and injuries, ranging from minor to more severe. Skin damage can include:

Abrasions and grazes

Abrasions or grazes refer to injuries where the top layer of skin is scraped or rubbed away due to friction against a rough surface. They are common on the knees, elbows and hands in sport. Ways of reducing the risk of abrasions and grazes include wearing protective clothing and avoiding rough surfaces.

Example: In tennis, a player may get abrasions or grazes when making dynamic moves, such as diving or sliding, especially on the knees and elbows, due to contact with a hard-court surface during intense rallies.

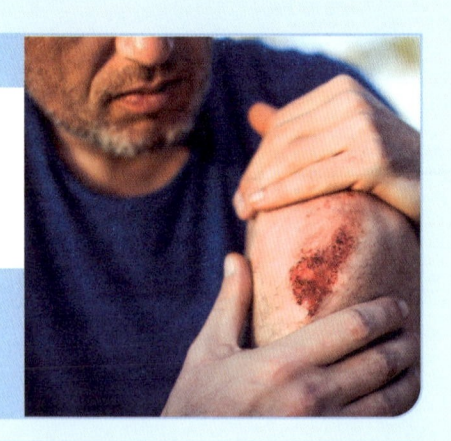

Cuts and lacerations

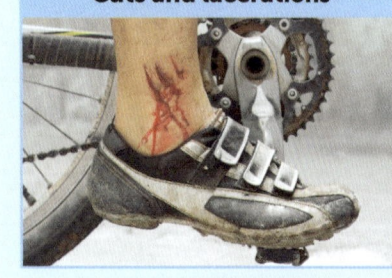

Cuts and lacerations are injuries that result in a break or opening of the skin. They can vary in severity, from small, **superficial** cuts to deeper wounds. They are common on areas prone to impact. Ways of reducing the risk of cuts and lacerations in sport are to wear protective equipment, such as helmets and gloves and by inspecting playing surfaces to remove any hazards.

Example: In cycling, a fall or close contact with rocks or thorny vegetation may cause cuts or grazes.

Superficial refers to an injury that affects only the outermost layer of tissue, such as the skin or the surface of a muscle.

Contusions

Contusions are more commonly known as **bruises**. They occur when blood vessels beneath the skin rupture. They can vary in size and colour, typically starting as red or purple and gradually changing to green or yellow as the body heals. They are common on the shins, knees, elbows, and hands in sport. Ways of reducing the risk of contusions in sport are to wear protective gear such as pads, helmets, and guards to shield vulnerable areas of the body from impact.

Example: In hockey, bruises can occur due to accidental stick or ball contact, especially in a crowded area. In boxing, bruises (and cuts) often occur, especially around the eyes owing to forceful punches.

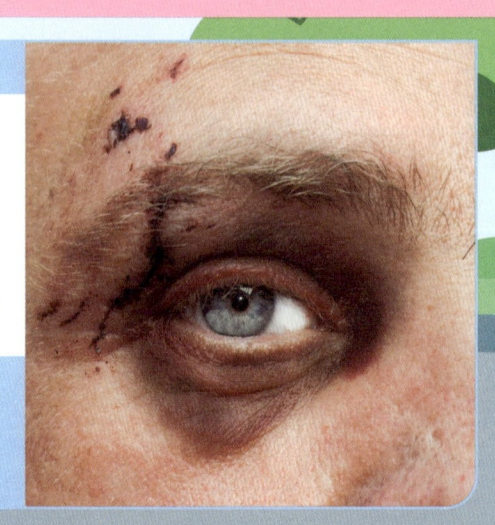

Blisters

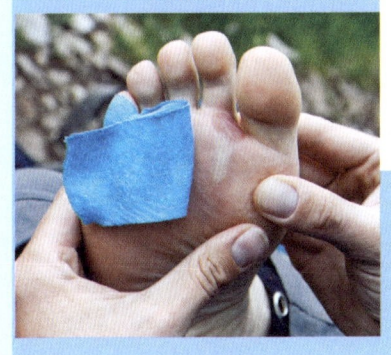

Blisters are fluid filled sacs that form on the skin's surface due to friction, pressure, or burns. They often appear as raised, swollen areas and can be filled with clear fluid or blood. They are common on the feet and heels in sport. Ways of reducing the risk of blisters in sport is to wear appropriate footwear that provides proper support and reduces friction.

Example: In cricket, a fielder may be wearing inappropriate or poorly fitting shoes. As the fielder repeatedly moves, sprints, or changes direction to field the ball, the friction between their feet and the footwear for the long duration of the game, will lead to blisters on the feet and heels.

Injury	Causes	Symptoms	Treatment (See Topic Area 4)
Abrasions or grazes	Friction, scraping against a rough surface	Superficial skin damage, bleeding	Cleaning, antiseptic, bandaging, wound care
Cuts and lacerations	Sharp objects, trauma	Bleeding, pain, visible wound	Cleaning, antiseptic, stitches, wound care
Contusions (bruises)	Impact, blunt force	Discoloration, pain, swelling	Cold compress, elevation, pain relief
Blisters	Friction, pressure, rubbing	Fluid filled sac, pain, redness	Avoidance of further friction, blister care, bandaging

Describe **two** differences between a bruise and a blister. [4]

A bruise is cause by an impact,[1] a blister is caused by friction/rubbing.[1] / A bruise is an injury that damages small blood vessels beneath the skin,[1] a blister leads to the separation of the outermost layer of skin from the underlying layers.[1] / A bruise will have discoloured skin,[1] a blister will have a fluid filled sac on the surface of the skin.[1]

3.1.6–3.1.7

FRACTURES AND DISLOCATIONS

Participating in sports exposes individuals to the risk of both open and closed fractures. These injuries occur when bones are subject to high forces, often from impact collisions or falls.

Fractures

Open fractures are characterised when a bone pierces through the skin. **Closed fractures** are where the skin remains intact. Both open and closed fractures are common to the bones in the arms and legs, but open fractures increase the risk of infection. Ways of reducing the risk of fractures is to use protective gear and compete in a safe manner.

Compare acute fractures with stress fractures on **page 40**.

Example: In gymnastics, a gymnast is performing a series of complex back handsprings on the floor. During one of these skills, they miscalculate the landing and over rotate, leading to an awkward landing with excessive force on an outstretched leg. The impact, combined with the high force generated during back handsprings, could result in a fracture of the lower leg bone.

Injury	Causes	Symptoms	Treatment (See Topic Area 4)
Open fractures	Trauma, direct impact	Visible bone, bleeding, deformity	Immobilisation, emergency medical attention, surgery
Closed fractures	Trauma, direct impact	Pain, swelling, possible deformity	Immobilisation, medical assessment, possible surgery

Dislocations

A **dislocation** occurs when the normal alignment of bones at a joint is disrupted. Dislocations can result from traumatic incidents, such as falls or impacts, and commonly affect joints in the shoulders, fingers, elbows, or knees. Ways of reducing the risk of dislocations are to complete strengthening exercises, use proper sporting technique and wear protective gear.

Example: In netball, a Goal Defence is jumping to intercept a pass from an opponent. During the jump, the GD contacts another player and then lands awkwardly on one foot, resulting in a sudden and forceful impact. The impact combined with the awkward landing, could potentially lead to a dislocation at the ankle joint.

Causes	Symptoms	Treatment (See Topic Area 4)
Forceful impact, joint instability	Deformity, severe pain, limited movement	Immobilisation, medical attention, possible surgery

A Rugby player has been injured. A bone in their lower leg has pierced the skin and is bleeding heavily. State the type of injury that they have sustained. [1]

Open fracture.[1]

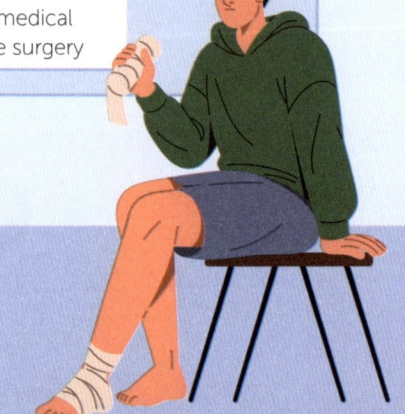

3.1.8

HEAD INJURIES

Head injuries encompass a spectrum of traumatic events affecting both the skull and the brain, ranging from mild concussion to more severe conditions, including the potential onset of dementia and Alzheimer's disease.

Concussion

Concussion specifically involves traumatic impact to the brain, causing a temporary disruption of normal brain function. Furthermore, a growing body of evidence suggests a potential link between repetitive head injuries and an increased risk of developing **dementia** and **Alzheimer's**. Ways of reducing the risk of head injuries are to wear head protection, adhere to rules and regulations about head impact and compete in a safe manner.

Dementia is a general term describing a decline in mental ability, including memory loss and cognitive impairment.

Alzheimer's disease is a progressively neurodegenerative disorder characterised by memory loss, cognitive decline, and behavioural changes, affecting the brain's function over time.

Example: In rugby, a concussion may occur during a tackle when a player's head makes direct, forceful contact with an opponent's body or the ground.

Injury	Causes	Symptoms	Treatment
Concussion	Head impact	Headache, confusion, dizziness	Rest, medical assessment, gradual return to activity
Head injuries and the onset of dementia and Alzheimer's	Repeated head trauma, concussion	Memory loss, cognitive decline	Monitoring, early intervention, neurological assessments

During a football match, a player sustains a blow to the head after colliding with an opponent. Which **one** of the following signs would the player display shortly after the impact, suggesting a possible concussion? [1]

A - Bruising and swelling at the point of impact

B - Disorientation and a brief loss of balance

C - Rapid heartbeat and increased blood pressure

D - Tingling sensation in the fingers and toes

B - Disorientation and a brief loss of balance.[1]

OCR Cambridge Nationals **Sport Science** – R180: Topic Area 3

3.2.1

CHRONIC INJURIES

Participating in sports provides a sense of fulfilment, healthy competition, and joy, yet it is accompanied by the potential threat of chronic injuries, which can significantly impact the ability to participate in the long term.

Overview of chronic injuries

Unlike the sudden nature of acute injuries, **chronic injuries develop gradually over time** and may result from repetitive stress or prolonged strain on specific areas of the body, ranging in severity from mild to enduring.

> Chronic injuries are named after the Greek word for time, *'chrono'*.

Overuse

Overuse injuries occur when a specific part of the body is subjected to repetitive stress without sufficient time for recovery. Overuse injuries can affect various tissues, such as muscles, tendons, and bones. They are a common concern in sports where repetitive motions are frequent.

Example: In long-distance running, runners who gradually increase their mileage without allowing adequate time from recovery may be prone to overuse injuries in the ankles, shins, knees and hips.

Symptoms	Treatment
Persistent pain in the affected area, swelling and inflammation, decreased range of motion, and weakness.	Rest, reduce activity, ice therapy, stretching, strengthening, cross-training, and anti-inflammatory medication.

Develop gradually over a period of time

Chronic injuries develop over weeks, months or even years and can stem from a combination of factors, including **biomechanical** issues, incorrect training techniques, or inadequate rest periods.

> **Biomechanical** refer to an individual's movement patterns and body mechanics.

Example: In swimming, over time, continuous stress put on a shoulder joint, combined with improper technique can lead to the gradual onset of 'swimmer's shoulder'.

Symptoms	Treatment
Persistent dull pain in the affected area, gradual onset of discomfort during physical activity, swelling and inflammation after prolonged activity, limited flexibility and tenderness.	Rest, reduce activity, physical therapy for targeted exercise, ice therapy, massage therapy.

Repetitive movement

Repetitive movements play a significant role in the occurrence of chronic injuries. Performers engaged in activities that involve repeated motions, such as running, cycling or overhead throwing, are at greater risk, due to the consistent stress placed on specific joints and tissues.

Example: In cycling, the repetitive nature of the leg movement involved with pedalling, places consistent stress on the knee joints and surrounding tissues.

Symptoms	Treatment
Persistent pain in the affected area, gradual onset of discomfort during specific movements, tenderness after repetitive actions, swelling and inflammation in specific joints, limited range of motion and weakness in muscles.	Rest, modification of activities to reduce repetition, physical therapy for targeted exercise, ice therapy, stretching and flexibility exercise.

Ways of reducing risk of chronic injuries

Reducing the risk of chronic injuries in sport involves a combination of proactive measures aimed at promoting overall well-being and minimising the factors that contribute to long-term damage. Some strategies to help lessen the risk of chronic injuries include:

- Proper warm-up and cool-down
- Gradual intensity progression
- Proper technique
- Appropriate equipment
- Strength and flexibility training
- Rest and recovery

---

1. Which **one** of the following are often the cause of overuse injuries in sports? [1]
   A - Adequate rest intervals
   B - Dynamic stretching exercise
   C - Proper warm-up routines
   D - Sudden increases in training intensity

2. Bonnie is a long-distance runner who has been experiencing gradual pain in her knees. Identify **one** possible cause for her condition and suggest **one** preventative measure. [2]

---

1. D – Sudden increases in training intensity.[1]

2. Overuse due to the repetitive nature of running,[1] incorporate cross-training activities.[1] / Biomechanical issues in her running form,[1] improve her running technique.[1] / Inadequate rest and recovery,[1] ensure sufficient rest intervals.[1]

3.2.2

TENDONITIS

Tendonitis is a chronic sporting injury that involves inflammation of tendons; the connective tissue that attaches muscles to bone. Tendonitis often occurs from repetitive movements, overuse, or biomechanical issues and can impact various joints in the body.

Achilles tendonitis

Achilles tendonitis involves inflammation of the **Achilles tendon**, that connects the calf muscle to the heel bone. This condition is commonly seen in athletes engaged in activities requiring frequent pushing off the foot, such as **running** or **jumping**.

Rotator cuff tendonitis

Rotator cuff tendonitis involves inflammation of the tendons surrounding the shoulder joint. Athletes participating in sports that requires repetitive overhead movements such as **throwing** or **swimming**, are particularly prone to the condition.

Patellar tendonitis

Patellar tendonitis, also known as jumpers' knee, affects the tendon connecting the kneecap to the shinbone. This condition is common in sports involving frequent jumping and sudden stops, such as those movements in **basketball** or **volleyball**.

Injury	Causes	Symptoms	Treatment
Achilles tendonitis	Repetitive stress on the Achilles tendon	Pain and stiffness in the back of the heel, swelling, and difficulty walking	Rest, ice, compression, elevation, physical therapy, and in severe cases, possible surgery
Rotator cuff tendonitis	Overuse or repetitive overhead movements	Shoulder pain, weakness, limited range of motion, and discomfort while lifting the arm	Rest, ice, anti-inflammatory medications, physical therapy
Patellar tendonitis	Jumping and sudden stops	Pain around the kneecap, swelling, tenderness, and difficulty bending / straightening the knee	Rest, ice, compression, elevation, strengthening exercises

> Describe how tendonitis can occur at the knee joint. Give a sporting example in your answer. [2]
>
> *The continuous or repetitive use of the knee joint,[1] e.g. kicking a ball in football / when running long distance in athletics / when completing numerous squats in weightlifting.[1]*

3.2.3

EPICONDYLITIS

Epicondylitis describes the inflammation of tendons near the bony part of the elbow. Often stemming from repetitive movements, overuse, or improper technique, it can impact athletes involved with activities requiring repetitive gripping and arm movements.

Lateral epicondylitis (Tennis elbow)

Lateral epicondylitis, commonly known as **tennis elbow**, affects the outer part of the elbow. This is common in racquet sports, such as tennis or badminton, where repetitive wrist extension and gripping are frequent.

Medial epicondylitis (Golfers' elbow)

Medial epicondylitis, commonly referred to as **golfers' elbow**, affects the inner part of the elbow. This is common in sports involving forceful and repetitive wrist flexion, such as golf or baseball.

Injury	Causes	Symptoms	Treatment
Lateral epicondylitis (Tennis elbow)	Repetitive wrist extension and gripping movements	Pain in the outer part of the elbow, weakened grip strength, and discomfort during wrist movement	Protection, rest, ice, compression, elevation, anti-inflammatory medications, physical therapy, and bracing
Medial epicondylitis (Golfers elbow)	Forceful and repetitive wrist flexion	Pain on the inner part of the elbow, difficulty with wrist and hand movements, and weakened grip	

1. What is the primary cause of lateral epicondylitis? [1]
   - A - Forceful wrist flexion
   - B - Impact to the outer part of the elbow
   - C - Overhead throwing movements
   - D - Repetitive wrist extension and gripping
2. Explain the relationship between epicondylitis and chronic sporting injuries [2]

---

1. D – Repetitive wrist extension and gripping.[1]
2. Chronic injuries develop over time and may result from repetitive movements or overuse on specific areas of the body.[1] Epicondylitis involves inflammation of tendons near the elbow joint due to repetitive stresses put on the joint in sports such as tennis or golf.[1]

3.2.4–3.2.5

SHIN SPLINTS AND STRESS FRACTURES

Shin splints are a common form of chronic injury in sports, particularly those involving repetitive impact or stress on the lower leg. Stress fractures are also typically caused by repetitive stress and overuse, and are characterised by small cracks or fractures in bones (**see page 34**).

Shin splints

Shin splints are characterised by pain along the inner edge of the tibia (shinbone) and are often associated with activities including running, jumping, or those that involve sudden stops and starts. Ways of reducing the risk of shin splints are to wear proper footwear with appropriate arch support and cushioning, ensure a gradual return to activity after symptoms lessen, stretch the calf muscles and strengthen the lower leg to improve flexibility and support.

Example: A cross country runner can generate stress on the shinbone and surrounding tissue through repeated impact on uneven ground, making the athlete more susceptible to shin splints.

Causes	Symptoms	Treatment
Overuse, biomechanical issues, training errors	Pain, tenderness, increased pain with activity	Protection, rest, ice and compression, anti-inflammatory medication

Stress fractures

Stress fractures are common in weight bearing bones and are prevalent in sports that involve repetitive impact, such as running, jumping and activities with sudden stops and starts. Stress fractures develop gradually over time. Ways of reducing stress fractures are to gradually increase training intensity to allow bones time to adapt, wear appropriate footwear that provides support and cushioning, and allow sufficient time for rest and recovery between periods of intense activity.

Example: Volleyball players often engage in repetitive jumping, sudden stops, and forceful landings, placing significant stress on their lower legs, increasing the risk of stress fractures.

Causes	Symptoms	Treatment
Repetitive stress, training errors, poor technique, poor nutrition	Pain, swelling, tenderness to touch, pain during weight bearing activities	Protection, rest, immobilisation, gradual return to activity

Explain the difference between an acute and a chronic injury. [2]

An acute injury is characterised by a sudden and immediate onset, often resulting from a specific traumatic accident.[1] A chronic injury develops gradually over an extended period of time. / Its onset is slow and gradual.[1]

Topic Area 3

EXAMINATION PRACTICE

Topic area 3: Different types and causes of sports injuries

1. Which **one** of the following sports is most commonly associated with the development of stress fractures? [1]
   - ☐ A – Cycling
   - ☐ B – Long jump
   - ☐ C – Swimming
   - ☐ D – Table tennis

2. Paddy is a competitive tennis player who has been experiencing persistent pain in his elbow during and after matches.

   (a) State the chronic injury Paddy may be suffering from. [1]

   (b) Outline **one** potential causes of this injury. [1]

   (c) Suggest **two** specific preventative measures and / or modifications to Paddy's training routine to manage and reduce the risk of the injury reoccurring. [2]

3. Complete the table below by identifying a common symptom and treatment for the injuries listed. [4]

Injury	Symptom	Treatment
Cut	(a)	(b)
Blisters	(c)	(d)

4. Compare and contrast the causes, symptoms, and treatments of Lateral epicondylitis (tennis elbow) and shin splints. [4]

5. Soft and hard tissue injuries are common in football.

   Analyse each injury type, highlighting the potential causes, symptoms, and treatment options associated with these injuries in the context of football. [8]

4.1.1

SAFETY CHECKS

Prioritising a safe and secure environment for sport and physical activity involves taking a proactive approach before and during play. Embracing the adage that *'prevention is better than cure'*, various measures can be adopted to reduce the risk and severity of injuries associated with sports participation.

Ensuring safety

Ensuring safety before and during participation in sports and physical activities involves a series of safety checks and measures to minimise the risk and severity of injuries and medical conditions (see **pages 29-40**).

Risk assessments

A **risk assessment** is a process of evaluating potential **risks** and **hazards** associated with a particular sporting activity, environment, or situation. The goal of a risk assessment is to identify, analyse, and prioritise risks so that appropriate measures can be taken to ease or manage them effectively.

> **Risk** is the likelihood or probability of harm. A **hazard** refers to something that can cause harm.

The following steps should be taken when completing a risk assessment:

1. Identify potential hazards in a sporting environment.
2. Assess the likelihood and severity of the risks associated with each hazard.
3. Determine and implement control measures to manage identified risks.
4. Comply with sports regulation and guidelines.
5. Establish emergency response plans for injuries or accidents.
6. Review and update the risk assessment based on changes and improvements.

Level of risk

Level of risk refers to the degree of potential harm or consequences associated with an event, based on two key factors:

- The likelihood of an event occurring
- The severity of its potential impact

42 ClearRevise

Levels of risk are categorised into three classifications

Level of risk	Description	Sporting example
Low	The likelihood of an event occurring is minimal. Consequences, if the event occurs, are minor.	Walking or jogging on a well-maintained track with proper lighting and clear pathways. The likelihood of injury is minimal, and consequences, if any, are likely to be minor.
Medium	There is a notable likelihood of an event happening. Consequences, if the event occurs, may range from moderate to significant.	Playing a non-contact sport such as tennis or badminton. While the risk of injury is moderate, with sprains or minor impacts possible, proper equipment and adherences to rules can help manage the risks.
High	There is a substantial likelihood of an event occurring. Consequences, if the event occurs, are severe or significant.	Competitive contact sports such as rugby or hockey. These sports involve a high likelihood of collisions and physical contact, increasing the risk of injuries such as fractures, concussions, or dislocations.

Characteristics of the individual/group

Prior to participating in sports, the **characteristics of both individuals and groups** involved should be assessed to ensure a safe experience. Some key considerations include:

- Age of participants
- Medical conditions
- Skill level
- Fitness level
- Previous injuries
- Experience

Group size

Group size considerations play an important role when completing a risk assessment. A crowded sports hall will increase the risk of collisions in contrast to a sports hall with only two individuals. Similarly, the risk level substantially decreases in a swimming session with a single participant compared to a pool filled with people.

Explain the difference between a hazard and a risk. Give **one** example of each in the context of football. [4]

A hazard refers to a potential source of harm or danger.[1] An example of a hazard could be an uneven playing field.[1] A risk refers to the likelihood of harm arising from the hazard.[1] An example would be the probability of a player tripping and getting injured due to the uneven playing field / likely severity of resulting injury.[1]

4.1.2

STRATEGIES TO HELP REDUCE THE RISK OF SPORTS INJURIES AND MEDICAL CONDITIONS

Participating in sports offers numerous health benefits, but the risk of injuries and medical conditions is ever-present. Effective **strategies** are vital to reduce these risks and maintain long-term well-being.

A **strategy** is a set of actions aimed at preventing or minimising the likelihood of injuries.

Medicals

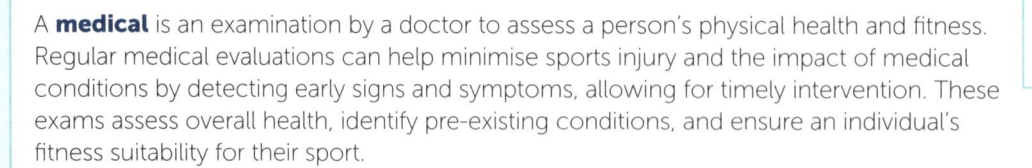

A **medical** is an examination by a doctor to assess a person's physical health and fitness. Regular medical evaluations can help minimise sports injury and the impact of medical conditions by detecting early signs and symptoms, allowing for timely intervention. These exams assess overall health, identify pre-existing conditions, and ensure an individual's fitness suitability for their sport.

Screening

In sport, **screening** can identify factors that contribute to sports injuries. Athletes undergo assessments to pinpoint weaknesses, allowing for targeted interventions such as specific training or corrective exercises. Regular screening allows athletes to optimise performance safely and prevent injuries. Screening can examine:

- Muscle imbalances
- Muscular strength
- Joint range of movement
- Joint stability
- Posture and alignment
- Bone density

National Governing Body (NGB) policies

Adhering to **National Governing Body (NGB)** policies is vital for creating a safe and secure sporting environment. These policies set out rules and regulations that govern various aspects such as fair play, proper equipment use, and injury prevention measures. In rugby, the Rugby Football Union (RFU) has implemented specific strategies, including tackling techniques, concussion protocols, and equipment standards to effectively reduce the risk of injuries.

Identify **one** rule or regulation implemented by a National Governing Body (NGB) as a preventive measure to reduce the risk of injury in its sport. [1]

The FA, no tackles from behind.[1] / *England Hockey, mandatory helmets for goalkeepers.*[1] / *England Boxing, mandatory gumshields to be worn.*[1]

4.1.3

EMERGENCY ACTION PLANS (EAP)

An **Emergency Action Plan (EAP)** is a written strategy that outlines the necessary steps and procedures to be followed in the event of an emergency during sport or physical activity. The primary goal of an EAP is to ensure the prompt and effective response to injuries or medical conditions, minimising the risk and severity of potential harm. An EAP has three parts:

Emergency personnel

In case of an emergency, it is crucial to be aware of which specific personnel to contact and the appropriate means of communication. The key individuals to be mindful of in an emergency include **first responders**, on-site **first aiders**, and, when necessary, **paramedics**.

Emergency communication

The EAP should include information about **emergency communication**, including relevant contact numbers for emergency services and any on-site specialised provisions such as the use of a public announcement (PA) system.

Emergency equipment

The EAP must detail on-site **emergency equipment** and its specific location. Essential emergency supplies include, but are not limited to, **first aid kits**, **AEDs**, **emergency medications**, **wheelchairs**, **stretchers**, **splints**, **ice packs** and **emergency blankets**.

Give **one** example for each section of an emergency action plan (EAP). [3]

EAP Section	Example
Emergency personnel	(a)
Emergency communication	(b)
Emergency equipment	(c)

Answers may include: (a) First responder / first aider / paramedic.[1] (b) Emergency services / 999 / PA System.[1] (c) First aid kit / AED (Automated External Defibrillator) / wheelchairs.[1]

OCR Cambridge Nationals **Sport Science** – R180: Topic Area 4

4.2.1

SALTAPS ON-FIELD ASSESSMENT ROUTINE

In sport, injuries are inevitable, requiring swift and effective responses for optimal recovery. Managing injuries in sport start with on-field assessments, leading to subsequent treatments and rehabilitation that address immediate concerns. They also ensure an athlete's long-term well-being, helping them to return to action.

SALTAPS

SALTAPS is an acronym for **See**, **Ask**, **Look**, **Touch**, **Active**, **Passive** and **Strength**. It is commonly used in first aid to remember the steps to assess and manage injuries, particularly musculoskeletal injuries that may occur in sport.

S	**See**	See the injury and stop the activity immediately. Ask what happened. Look at the injured person's face, body and behaviour.
A	**Ask**	Ask the injured person about the incident, including what happened, the nature of the pain, and any previous injuries or medical conditions.
L	**Look**	Inspect the injured area looking for any signs of deformity, swelling, bleeding or bruising.
T	**Touch**	Gently touch the injured area to assess for a response, tenderness, warmth, or other abnormalities.
A	**Active**	Ask the injured person if they can move the injured area and if they feel any pain.
P	**Passive**	If the 'Active' phase is ok, gently move the injured limb or joint through the full range of movement and check for any signs of pain.
S	**Strength**	Test for function. Depending on the injured area, ask the injured person to bear weight, grip something, push, pull or lift an object.

Describe **one** situation in sport where the SALTAPS method would be used. [2]

If there was an injury in a basketball game,[1] the SALTAPS method would be used to assess and respond to the incident.[1] / If an individual were to experience a medical condition in a netball match,[1] the SALTAPS methods would be used to assess and respond to the medical condition.[1]

4.2.2

DRABC

DRABC (or '**D**octo**r ABC**') is an acronym for **Danger, Response, Airway, Breathing** and **Circulation**. It is used in first aid and emergency responses. It is used to guide individuals through the necessary steps in assessing and providing initial care for injuries and medical conditions.

D — **Danger**
Before approaching an injured person, ensure that the surrounding area is safe for both the victim and yourself. Identify and eliminate any potential hazards that may pose a threat to safety.

R — **Response**
Check for a response from the person. Gently tap them and ask loudly if they are ok. Look for any signs of movement, breathing or responsiveness. If the person is unconscious, emergency services should be called.

A — **Airway**
Ensure that the person's airway is clear and unobstructed. If they are unconscious, gently tilt their head backward and lift the chin to open the airways. Check for any obstructions and remove carefully if present.

B — **Breathing**
Assess the person's breathing. Look, listen, and feel for signs of breathing. If they are not breathing, or if breathing is irregular or inadequate, initiate rescue breaths if trained to do so.

C — **Circulation**
Check for signs of circulation, such as a pulse. If there is no pulse and the person is not breathing, start **CPR**. If trained, use an automated external defibrillator (AED) if available.

CPR stands for **Cardiopulmonary Resuscitation**. It involves a combination of chest compressions and rescue breaths to help circulate blood and oxygen throughout the body.

4.2.3

RECOVERY POSITION

The recovery position is a first aid technique used to place an unconscious but breathing person with no other life-threatening condition or back injury, on their side. The position helps keep their airway clear and allows any fluids (saliva, vomit etc.) to drain from the mouth.

Placing someone in the recovery position

Placing someone in the recovery position is important to prevent choking and to maintain an open airway, especially if they are unable to maintain consciousness on their own. The general steps for placing someone in the recovery position are:

1. **Kneel down beside the person:** Ensure the person is lying on their back, and you are on one side of their body.

2. **Move the arm closest to you:** Extend the person's arm that is closest to you at a right angle to their body, with the palm facing up. Move the back of their other hand onto their cheek.

3. **Bring the far knee towards you:** Bend the person's far knee (the one furthest from you) to a right angle.

4. **Roll the person towards you:** Carefully roll the person on their side by gently pulling on the bent knee. Ensure their hand is supporting their head to maintain an open airway.

5. **Adjust the upper leg:** Position the person's upper leg so that it is in line with their hip, preventing them from rolling forwards or backwards.

6. **Check the airway:** Confirm that the person's airway remains clear and open. Tilt the head slightly backwards to ensure the airway is unobstructed.

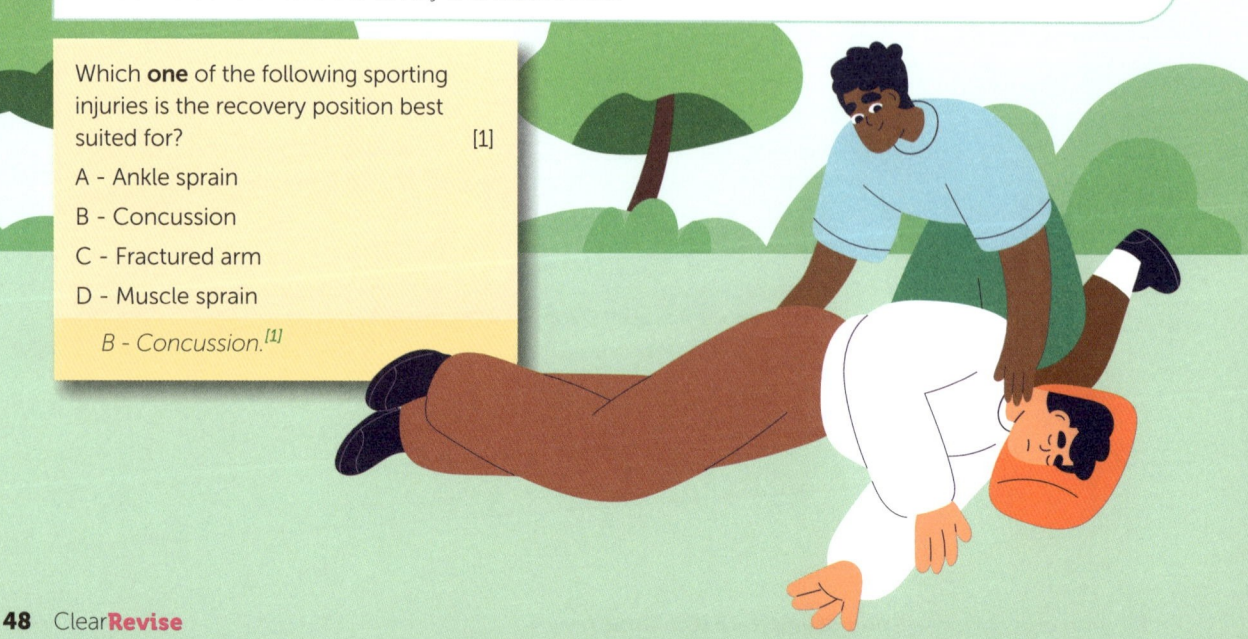

Which **one** of the following sporting injuries is the recovery position best suited for? [1]

A - Ankle sprain

B - Concussion

C - Fractured arm

D - Muscle sprain

B - Concussion.[1]

4.2.4

PRICE THERAPY

PRICE is an acronym for **Protection**, **Rest**, **Ice**, **Compress** and **Elevate** used in treating acute sporting injuries. It is commonly used with injuries such as sprains, strains, and other soft tissue injuries.

P	**Protect**	Protect the injured area from further harm. This may involve using a brace or splint to limit movement and prevent additional injury.
R	**Rest**	Give the injured area adequate time to heal by avoiding activities that may cause further damage.
I	**Ice**	Apply ice to the injured area for 15–20 minutes. This will help reduce pain, swelling and inflammation.
C	**Compress**	Apply compression to the injured area using an elastic bandage or compression wrap. This helps control swelling and provides support to the injured tissue.
E	**Elevate**	Elevate the injured area to minimise swelling. If possible, elevate the affected limb above the level of the heart when resting. This promotes fluid drainage and reduces swelling.

> State **two** benefits of applying ice to an injured area. [2]
>
> *Two from: Reduce pain.[1] / reduce swelling.[1] / reduce inflammation.[1]*

4.2.5

USE OF X-RAYS TO DETECT INJURY

X-rays play a crucial role in the detection of injuries in sport. They are commonly used to assess and identify skeletal injuries, such as fractures, dislocations and damage to growth plates.

Injuries seen through x-ray

You are not expected to know how x-rays work.

Fractures

X-rays are highly effective at revealing **fractures** in bones. Whether it is a fracture from overuse or a traumatic fracture resulting from an impact, x-rays provide detailed images that help diagnose and assess the severity of the break.

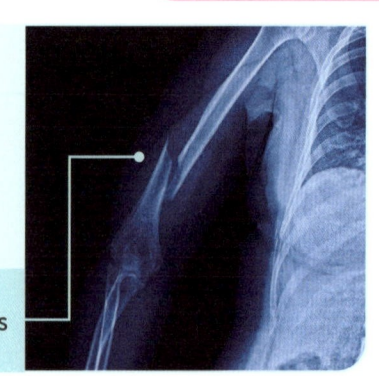

Fracture of the right humerus

Dislocations

X-rays are very helpful in detecting joint **dislocations**, where bones that normally articulate at a joint are displaced. This is particularly relevant in sports with a high risk of joint injuries, such as football or basketball.

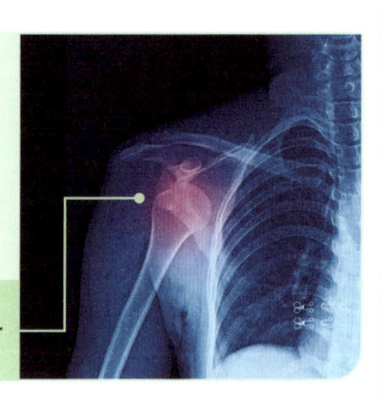

Dislocation of the right shoulder

Growth plates

Growth plates are areas of cartilage located at the end of bones in younger people, and are more vulnerable to injury than mature bone. X-rays are crucial in detecting injuries in growth plates, such as fracture or disruptions.

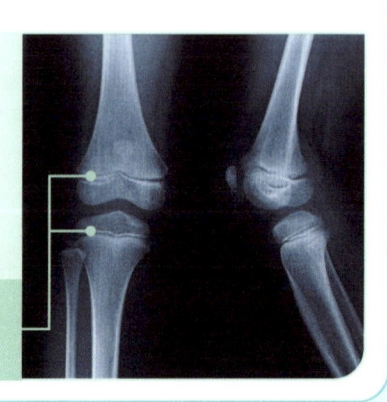

Growth plates on the right femur and tibia and fibula at the knee

4.2.6–4.2.7

OVERVIEW OF TREATMENTS AND THERAPIES

Injuries demand a range of treatments and therapies to ensure effective management and to aid a rapid recovery, restoring peak performance, and ensuring long-term well-being.

Treatment / Therapy	Benefit
Massage: Manual manipulation of soft tissues to alleviate muscle tension and enhance relaxation.	Increase blood flow, reduce muscle soreness, improve flexibility and relieve stress.
Ultrasound: High-frequency sound waves used to stimulate tissue repair.	Enhance healing, reduce inflammation, increase blood flow, improve tissue elasticity and alleviate pain.
Electrotherapy: Use of electrical currents for muscle stimulation and tissue repair.	Reduce pain, strengthen muscles, improve circulation and accelerate healing.
Hydrotherapy: Exercise and rehabilitation activities performed in water to reduce impact on joints.	Improve mobility, reduce pain and enhance circulation in a low-impact environment.
Cryotherapy: Exposure to extremely cold temperatures to promote healing.	Reduce pain and swelling, accelerate recovery, and improve muscle function.
Contrast therapy: Alternating between hot and cold treatments to promote healing.	Improve blood flow, reduce swelling, accelerate recovery and enhance tissue flexibility.
Painkillers: Medications, such as Ibuprofen, to alleviate pain and manage inflammation.	Temporary relief from pain, improve comfort during rehabilitation, and enhanced ability to participate in therapeutic exercises.
Support: Use of braces or tapes (Kinesiology taping, neoprene, bandaging) to support joints or muscles.	Joint stability, injury prevention, and support during recovery.
Immobilisation: Restriction of movement through casts, splints, or slings to promote healing and prevent further injury.	Stabilisation of injured areas, prevention of further damage, and support for tissue recovery.

Different psychological effects of dealing with injuries and medical conditions including treatment and long-term rehabilitation

Coping with injuries and medical conditions can profoundly impact an individual's psychological well-being throughout a long term treatment and rehabilitation process. See **page 12** for further details of psychological factors.

Exercise is known to release **endorphins** (feel good chemicals) that alleviate stress and anxiety. However, when an athlete is injured, the inability to exercise means a lack of endorphin release, potentially allowing psychological effects to worsen.

Implementing **mental strategies**, **(page 16)**, such as visualising the process of injury recovery, can help counteract the negative psychological effects.

4.2

RESPONSES AND TREATMENT OVERVIEW

Ensuring athlete well-being requires timely and strategic responses to injuries, along with appropriate treatments for medical conditions. The following table summarises this chapter.

Response or treatment	Advantage	Used for	Timing of response or treatment
SALTAPS	Systematic approach to assessing and treating injuries	Initial response to acute injuries	Immediately after injury
DRABC	Ensures proper steps for basic life support	Initial response to a medical emergency or severe injury	Immediately after injury
Recovery position	Maintains an open airway and aids breathing	Unconscious individuals or those with breathing difficulties	Immediately after injury
PRICE	Reduces inflammation and promotes healing	Acute injuries involving swelling and joint damage	Immediately after injury
X-rays	Provides detailed imaging of bones and structures	Suspected fractures or internal injuries	Immediately after injury
Massage	Enhances circulation, flexibility and relaxation	Muscle tension, soreness and preparation for performance	Prior to performance, during performance and during rehabilitation
Ultrasound	Promotes tissue healing and reduces inflammation	Soft tissue injuries and rehabilitation	During rehabilitation
Electrotherapy	Aids in pain management and muscle strengthening	Pain relief and muscle rehabilitation	During rehabilitation
Hydrotherapy	Facilities low-impact exercises and promotes recovery	Rehabilitation, flexibility and overall recovery	During rehabilitation
Cryotherapy	Reduces swelling and numbs pain	Acute injuries involving inflammation and pain	Immediately after injury
Contrast therapy	Promotes circulation and aids in muscle recovery	Rehabilitation and muscle recovery	During rehabilitation
Painkillers	Provides pain relief and reduces discomfort	Moderate to severe pain associated with injuries	As part of the longer-term rehabilitation process
Support	Stabilises injured areas and prevents further damage	Injuries requiring additional support or joint stability	Immediately after injury and as part of the longer-term rehabilitation process
Immobilisation	Restricts movement to promote healing	Fractures, severe sprains, or injuries requiring stability	Immediately after injury and as part of the longer-term rehabilitation process

During a high intensity football match, Daisy sustains a moderate ankle sprain after a sudden change in direction. The injury is characterised by swelling and pain in the affected ankle. You are the team's first aider.

Recommend the most appropriate and effective treatment for Daisy's ankle sprain. Justify your choice by referring to the advantages, uses, and timing of responses or treatments. [8]

The most effective treatment is the 'PRICE' protocol.[✓] PRICE, which stands for protection, rest, ice, compress, and elevate,[✓] offers several advantages that address the characteristics of a moderate ankle sprain.

Advantages of PRICE: *Reduces Inflammation[✓] – designed to address acute injuries involving swelling,[✓] making it ideal for a moderate ankle sprain. Promotes healing[✓] – by providing protection,[✓] rest, and targeted ice application. PRICE aids in the natural healing process of damaged tissues.[✓]*

Used for: *Acute injuries involving swelling and joint damage,[✓] precisely describing the nature of Daisy's moderate ankle sprain.*

Timing of response of treatment: *The PRICE protocol is recommended immediately after an injury[✓] and fits with the acute nature of the ankle sprain during the football match.[✓]*

Justification: *The acute nature of the ankle sprain, characterised by swelling and pain, makes the PRICE protocol the optimal choice. Applying immediate protection and rest, followed by targeted ice application, compression, and elevation, will effectively manage the inflammation,[✓] and promote the healing process.[✓] Moreover, administering PRICE aligns with the golden period immediately after injury, enhancing its effectiveness in reducing the severity[✓] of the sprain and helping Daisy's recovery. This approach ensures a comprehensive response to the injury and is in line with the best practice for acute soft tissue injuries in sport.[✓]*

Tick marks are used for guidance on valid points. This question should be marked in accordance with the mark scheme on page 82.

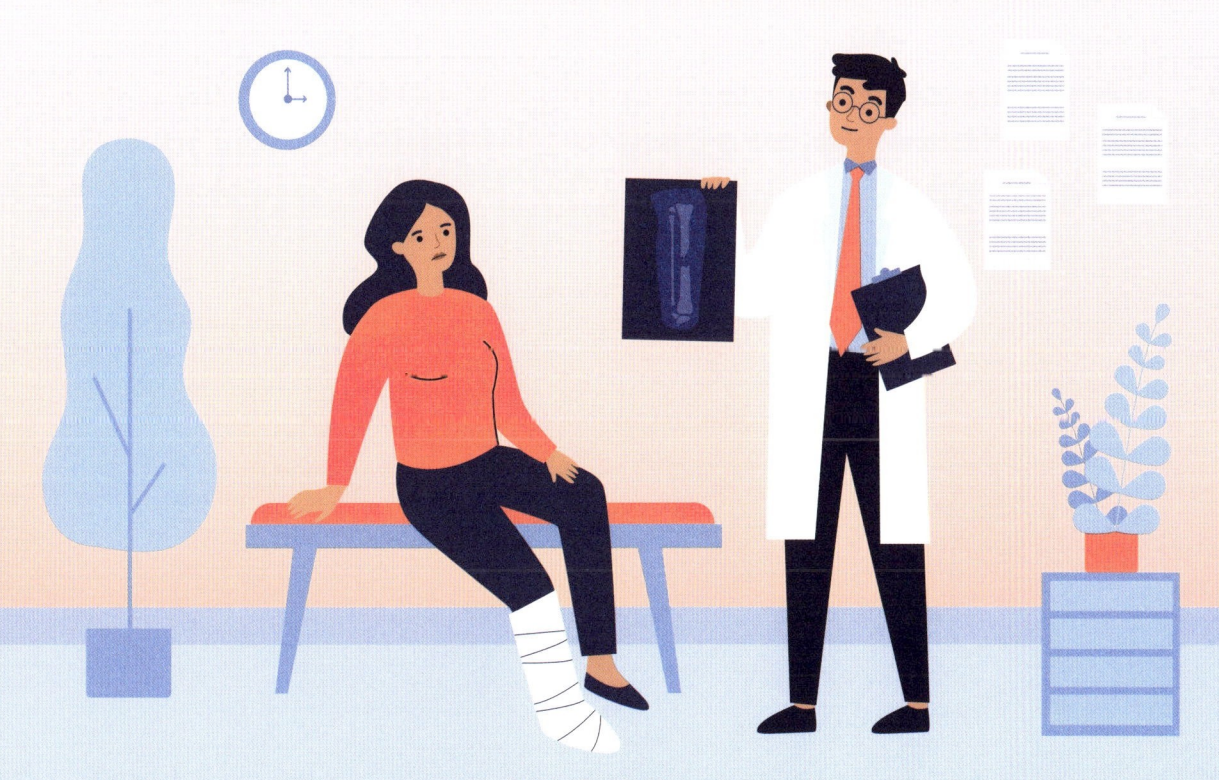

Topic Area 4

EXAMINATION PRACTICE

Topic area 4: Reducing risk, treatment and rehabilitation of sports injuries and medical conditions

1. Which **one** of the following is not part of an Emergency Action Plan (EAP)? [1]
   - ☐ A – Emergency communication
   - ☐ B – Emergency equipment
   - ☐ C – Emergency personnel
   - ☐ D – Emergency risk

2. Which **one** of the following therapies is commonly used for improving joint flexibility and reducing muscle soreness? [1]
   - ☐ A – Hydrotherapy
   - ☐ B – Immobilisation
   - ☐ C – Massage
   - ☐ D – Ultrasound

3. PRICE is an acronym used in treating acute sporting injuries. What does the 'P' stand for? [1]
   - ☐ A – Painkillers
   - ☐ B – Passive
   - ☐ C – Personnel
   - ☐ D – Protection

4. Risk assessments are completed before physical activities take place.
   - (a) Explain the purpose of a risk assessment. [2]
   - (b) Explain **two** ways in which the characteristics of a group affects the level of risk. [4]
   - (c) Explain how a medical examination before physical activity can reduce the level of risk. [2]

5. A person is found unconscious. *Breathing* represents step B of the DRABC acronym for first aid response.
   - (a) Describe what action is recommended as part of the *Breathing* step. [2]
   - (b) Explain the purpose of placing an unconscious, but breathing, person with no other life-threatening conditions into the recovery position. [2]

6. State **two** examples of sports injuries that can be effectively detected using X-rays. [2]

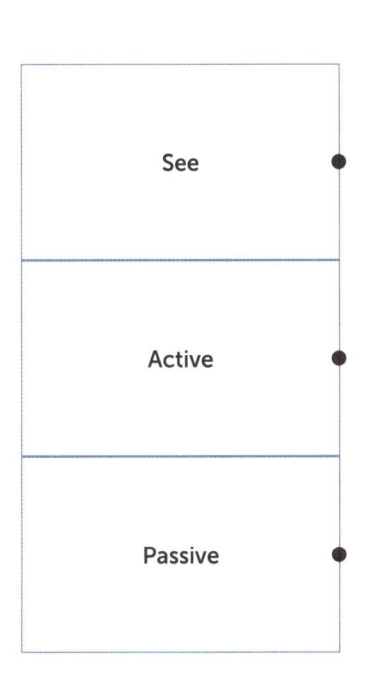

7. SALTAPS is an acronym used in first aid to assess and manage injuries.
Draw a straight line to match each part of SALTAPS to the correct description. [3]

SALTAPS part	Description
See	Gently move the injured limb or joint through the full range of movement.
Active	Ask if anybody saw what happened and stop the activity immediately.
Passive	Ask the injured person to stand and see if they can support their own weight.
	Ask the injured person if they can move the injured area.

8. Complete the table below by giving an overview of the sports treatment and a benefit of each to ensure effective management of sports injuries. [4]

Treatment	Overview	Benefit
Cryotherapy	(a)	(b)
Painkillers	(c)	(d)

9. Evaluate the use of hot and cold therapies in the treatment of sports injuries.

Include specific examples of when each therapy might be more appropriate. [8]

OCR Cambridge Nationals **Sport Science – R180: Topic Area 4**

5.1

ASTHMA

Asthma is a chronic breathing condition where the airways in and out of the lungs become narrower through inflammation, making it harder to breathe.

Causes and triggers

Causes and triggers of asthma attacks can be diverse, and they often vary from person to person.

A **chronic** condition is one that lasts for an extended period of time.

Environment:

Factors that contribute to an asthma attack can include allergens (such as pollen, dust mites and mould spores) or air quality (including smoke, pollution or fumes, cold or humid weather conditions and respiratory infections, such as the common cold or flu).

Exercise:

Some people have exercise-induced asthma that occurs during or after physical activity. Cold and dry air may act as a trigger, making it advantageous to breathe through the nose to warm the air, but this is hard to do especially when completing vigorous exercise.

Common symptoms

The four symptoms of asthma are listed by the NHS alongside their relevant guidance at www.nhs.uk

1. **Coughing:** A persistent cough is common. It may be worse at night or early in the morning.

2. **Wheezing:** A whistling or hissing sound during breathing, especially when exhaling. This noise results from the narrowing of the airways.

3. **Shortness of breath:** Individuals may experience a sensation of breathlessness. This can range from mild to severe, depending on the extent of airway constriction.

4. **Tightness in the chest:** Asthma can cause a feeling of tightness or pressure in the chest. This sensation may be accompanied by discomfort or pain.

Treatment

Reassurance

When reassuring someone, you must remain calm and take prompt action. Encourage them to sit up and lean forward slightly, taking slow, deep breaths. Loosen any tight clothing.

Inhalers

Inhalers are devices that deliver medication directly to the lungs, providing quick relief or long-term control of asthmatic symptoms. There are different types of inhalers: reliever, preventer, or combination inhalers.

Nebulisers

Nebulisers are devices that convert liquid medication into a fine mist or aerosol, allowing individuals to inhale the medication into their lungs through a mask.

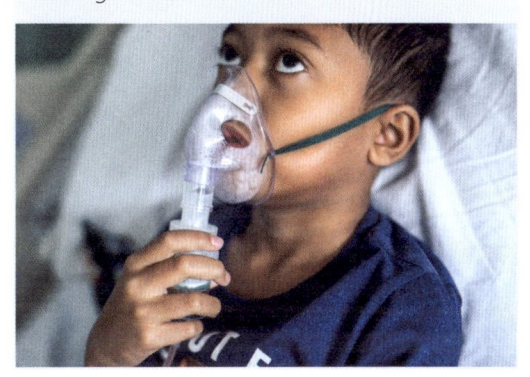

How to manage asthma when participating in sport or exercise

Individuals with asthma can participate in physical activities with proper management after consultation with a healthcare provider. Some simple tips for managing asthma during sports or exercise include:

- Be mindful of the environment
- Use an inhaler as prescribed
- Choose asthma-friendly activities
- Use a mask in cold weather
- Inform others
- Take breaks as needed
- Know your limits
- Stay hydrated
- Warm up

Jack is a keen young sports performer diagnosed with exercise-induced asthma. He is concerned about how his asthma may impact his performance and wants to ensure safe participation.

Explain **two** ways Jack can manage his asthma while participating in sport. [4]

Jack should perform a thorough warm up,[1] to gradually increase his heart rate and prepare his lungs for the physical activity.[1] / Jack should use his inhaler before physical activity,[1] to ensure his airways remain open during physical activity.[1]

5.2

DIABETES

Diabetes is a chronic medical condition characterised by elevated levels of **blood glucose** (sugar), which can lead to serious health complications. There are two types of diabetes (Type 1 and Type 2), both involving changes in the body's ability to produce **insulin**, a hormone produced by the pancreas that helps cells absorb glucose for energy.

> Blood glucose refers to the concentration of glucose (a type of sugar) present in the blood.

	Age and lifestyle	Causes
Type 1	**Type 1** diabetes is often diagnosed in children, adolescents, or young adults and is thought to be caused by genetics and factors in the environment.	**The body is unable to produce insulin.** The body's immune system mistakenly attacks and destroys insulin-producing cells in the pancreas. Without sufficient insulin, the body can not properly absorb glucose from the bloodstream into cells, leading to elevated blood sugar levels.
Type 2	**Type 2** diabetes is more common in adults, especially those over the age of 45. It is more likely to be caused by poor lifestyle choices, such as a lack of exercise, unhealthy diet, smoking, alcohol and stress.	**The body does not produce enough insulin, or insulin does not work properly.** The body's cells can become gradually more resistant to the effects of insulin causing the pancreas to produce more and more of it until it eventually can't keep up and blood glucose levels rise.

Common symptoms

1. **Increased thirst:** Elevated blood sugar levels can decrease the effectiveness of the kidneys causing excess sugar in the urine which causes **more frequent urination**. This causes dehydration (see **page 68**), creating a cycle where you need to drink more to compensate for fluid loss.

2. **Extreme tiredness:** Tiredness is caused by difficulties in efficiently converting glucose into energy, often caused by insulin-related issues. This can lead to long-term fatigue as cells struggle to get the energy they need.

3. **Weight loss:** As the body is less efficient at using glucose for energy, it starts to convert muscle and fat into energy instead, leading to weight loss.

4. **Cuts take a long time to heal:** Elevated blood sugar levels slow down the healing process, causing the skin to take longer to heal, repair and regenerate tissues.

> People with Type 1 Diabetes need to check their blood sugar regularly. This involves a simple process of pricking a finger to obtain a small blood sample, which is then measured using a handheld device called a blood glucose meter. The device provides an accurate reading of the level of sugar in the blood so they can make informed decisions about their diabetes management.

Treatment

Insulin / glucose: Individuals with Type 1 diabetes require insulin therapy as their pancreas does not produce insulin. This is usually administered through injections or by using an insulin pump.

Lifestyle changes: Adopting a healthy lifestyle including regular exercise and improving diet are recommended to help lose weight and reduce BMI. Avoiding stress will lower blood pressure.

Diet: Adopting a healthy diet is beneficial. This should be balanced with an emphasis on whole grains, fruits and vegetables, with limited sugars and processed foods.

Exercise: Regular physical activity helps improve insulin sensitivity and overall blood sugar control.

Monitoring

Regular monitoring of blood sugar levels is a crucial aspect of effective diabetes management, essential for preventing both **hypoglycaemia** and **hyperglycaemia**.

Hypoglycaemia (Hypo)

Commonly known as **low blood sugar**, a 'hypo' occurs when the level of glucose in the blood drops below the normal range.

Hyperglycaemia

Refers to **high blood sugar** levels in the bloodstream.

Compare and contrast hypoglycaemia and hyperglycaemia.
Include the key differences and similarities between them. [4]

Comparisons: Both are commonly associated with diabetes[1] / both involve the dysregulation of blood sugar levels.[1] **Contrasts:** Hypo involves low blood sugar[1] / hyper involves high blood sugar.[1]

How to manage diabetes when participating in sport or exercise

Managing diabetes during physical activity is essential to ensure optimal performance and prevent complications. Some guidelines for managing diabetes during physical activity include:

- Monitor blood sugar levels
- Carry fast-acting carbohydrates
- Wear medical identification
- Timing of meals
- Adjust insulin dosage
- Listen to your body
- Staying hydrated
- Correct type of exercise
- Post-exercise monitoring

5.3

EPILEPSY

Epilepsy is a common neurological condition characterised by abnormal brain activity, leading to recurrent, unprovoked **seizures** that can affect individuals of all ages and backgrounds.

> A seizure is a sudden and uncontrolled electrical disturbance in the brain

Common causes and triggers of epilepsy

The causes of epileptic seizures are not clearly understood. Approximately 1 in 3 individuals with epilepsy have a family history of the condition, suggesting a potential genetic link. Some people with epilepsy experience specific seizure **triggers**. Common causes and triggers include:

> Triggers are factors that can increase the likelihood of seizures occurring.

1. **Severe head injuries:** Epilepsy can result from brain damage which may, for example, be caused by strokes, brain tumours, infections, oxygen deprivation during birth, or head injuries sustained during sports or daily activities.

2. **Anxiety and stress:** These are not direct causes of epilepsy. However, they can act as triggers that may provoke seizures in some people who already have epilepsy.

3. **Tiredness and lack of sleep:** A side effect of anti-epileptic medication is fatigue, which is extreme tiredness. This can be significant trigger for seizures in people with epilepsy. Sleep plays a crucial role in maintaining overall brain health, and disruption to the sleep-wake cycle can lower the seizure threshold, making it more likely for seizures to occur.

Common symptoms

Eyes:

Staring blankly or **rapid blinking** and repetitive eye movements (**fluttering**) can occur during certain types of seizures.

Mouth:

People having a seizure are often unable to communicate and may **chew or bite** their tongue, cheek or lip. They may also have **slurred speech** or make **random noises**. Many also report an **unusual taste** in the mouth.

Limbs:

The arms and legs often experience a combination of **stiffness** and **uncontrollable movements** including **twitching** and **shaking** during a seizure.

Treatment

Anti-epileptic drugs (AEDs):

AEDs help manage seizures by altering brain chemical levels, serving as the primary treatment for epilepsy and successfully controlling seizures in approximately 7 out of 10 individuals.

> Careful not to confuse Anti-epileptic drugs (AEDs) with Automated External Defibrillators (AEDs).

Ketogenic diet:

The keto diet is classed as a medical treatment to help control seizures. It is a **high fat**, **low carbohydrate** diet that changes the chemical levels in the brain.

How to manage epilepsy when participating in sport or exercise

Exercise brings many health benefits to individuals with epilepsy and is rarely a trigger for seizures. However, some precautions should be taken with certain activities that include:

- Wear a MedicAlert bracelet
- Carry a MedicAlert card
- Avoid dangerous activities
- Avoid exercising alone
- Use a buddy system
- Drink plenty of fluids
- Take regular breaks
- Listen to your body
- Wear appropriate safety gear

---

1. Which **one** of the following is **not** a common symptom of epilepsy? [1]
   A – Making random noises
   B – Memory improvement
   C – Rapid eye movement
   D – Uncontrollable jerking

2. State **one** physical activity that individuals with epilepsy should try and avoid. Explain **one** reason for your choice of physical activity. [3]

---

1. B – Memory improvement.[1]

2. Answer include: Scuba diving,[1] due to the increased pressure on the brain[1] / which could trigger a seizure[1] / risk of seizure related complications underwater.[1] / Rock climbing,[1] as this activity increases the risk of potential falls with seizures at height[1] leading to serious injuries for the individual.[1]

5.4

SUDDEN CARDIAC ARREST (SCA)

Sudden Cardiac Arrest (SCA) occurs when the heart suddenly and unexpectedly stops beating due to a malfunction with the heart's electrical system. An SCA is different from a heart attack, which is caused when blood flow to part of the heart is blocked, usually by a blood clot.

Causes

An SCA causes an irregular heartbeat, which prevents the heart from pumping blood to the rest of the body. Several causes can contribute to a cardiac arrest, including:

Underlying genetic heart conditions:

Some people may have underlying (or undiagnosed) heart conditions, such as hypertrophic cardiomyopathy. This is thickening of the heart muscles and is a genetic condition.

Intense physical activity:

Intense and prolonged physical activity without enough rest and recovery can lead to overexertion, causing stress on the cardiovascular system. This can trigger an abnormal heart rhythm (arrhythmia).

Sudden trauma:

Severe trauma, such as a sudden blow to the chest, can disrupt the heart's electrical system.

Symptoms

Unconsciousness:

A SCA typically causes a sudden loss of responsiveness and consciousness. The person may collapse and become unresponsive.

Breathing difficulties:

Some people may experience chest pain or discomfort before an SCA. The person may stop breathing, or have difficulties breathing. They may gasp for air.

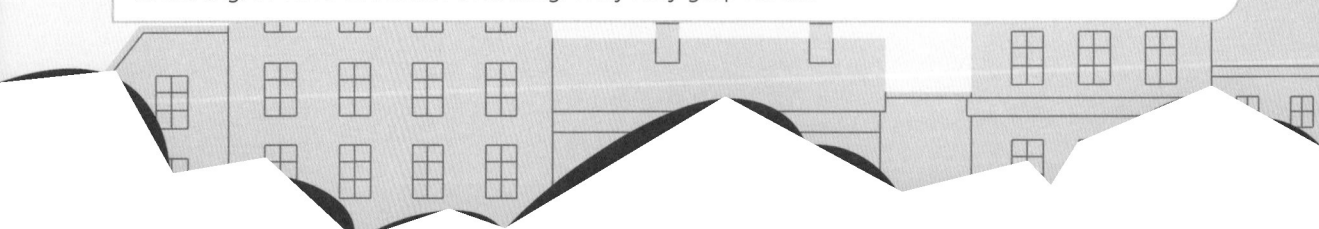

Treatment

An SCA can be fatal if not treated immediately.

Defibrillators:

This is a portable medical device called an **Automated External Defibrillator**, more commonly known as an **AED**. Requiring no formal training to operate, the AED delivers a controlled electric shock to the heart to restore normal cardiac rhythm.

Lifestyle changes:

Regular exercise, a healthy diet, maintaining a healthy weight, not smoking, limiting alcohol consumption, and managing stress can all play a role in preventing cardiovascular events that may contribute to an SCA.

---

1. What medical device is commonly used in the treatment of sudden cardiac arrest to deliver an electric shock and restore normal heart rhythm? [1]

   A – AED
   B – CGM
   C – CPAP
   D – MRI

2. Footballer, Christian Eriksen suffered a sudden cardiac arrest during a European Championship football match in 2021. Describe what is meant by a sudden cardiac arrest and explain how this differs from a heart attack. [4]

---

1. A – AED[1]
2. An SCA is a result of a sudden, severe disruption of the heart's electrical system,[1] causing an irregular heart rhythm / causing it to stop pumping blood.[1] A heart attack is a result of restricted blood flow through the heart,[1] usually caused by a blockage from a blood clot.[1]

5.5.1–5.5.4

HYPOTHERMIA

Hypothermia is a condition that occurs when the body loses heat faster than it can produce heat, causing the body temperature to drop below the normal range.

Causes of hypothermia

Hypothermia normally occurs in cold weather, but it can also develop in cool or windy conditions, especially if a person is wet.

Body temperature drops below 35°C

The normal body temperature is 37°C. If the body gets too cold and the core body temperature drops **below 35°C**, then hypothermia will occur.

Prolonged exposure to cold or wet conditions

Cold and windy conditions can contribute to the onset of hypothermia. **Wind** can increase heat loss from the body, making it feel colder than the actual air temperature. **Wet clothing** or exposure to water will increase heat loss as water conducts heat away from the body more efficiently than air, leading to a more rapid drop in body temperature. See **pages 6-8**.

---

1. Which **one** of the following factors can contribute to hypothermia? [1]
   A – Drinking hot drinks
   B – Exposure to cold and wet conditions
   C – Exposure to hot and humid conditions
   D – Wearing layered clothing

2. Fill in the table with appropriate preventative measures and treatments for hypothermia. [4]

	Preventive measures	Treatment
Clothing	(a)	(b)
Environment	(c)	(d)

---

1. B – Exposure to cold and wet conditions.[1]
2. (a) Wear layered clothing / avoid wet clothing.[1] (b) Rewarm gradually / use warm blankets.[1]
   (c) Stay dry / seek shelter from wind and cold.[1] (d) Move to a warmer place.[1]

Symptoms

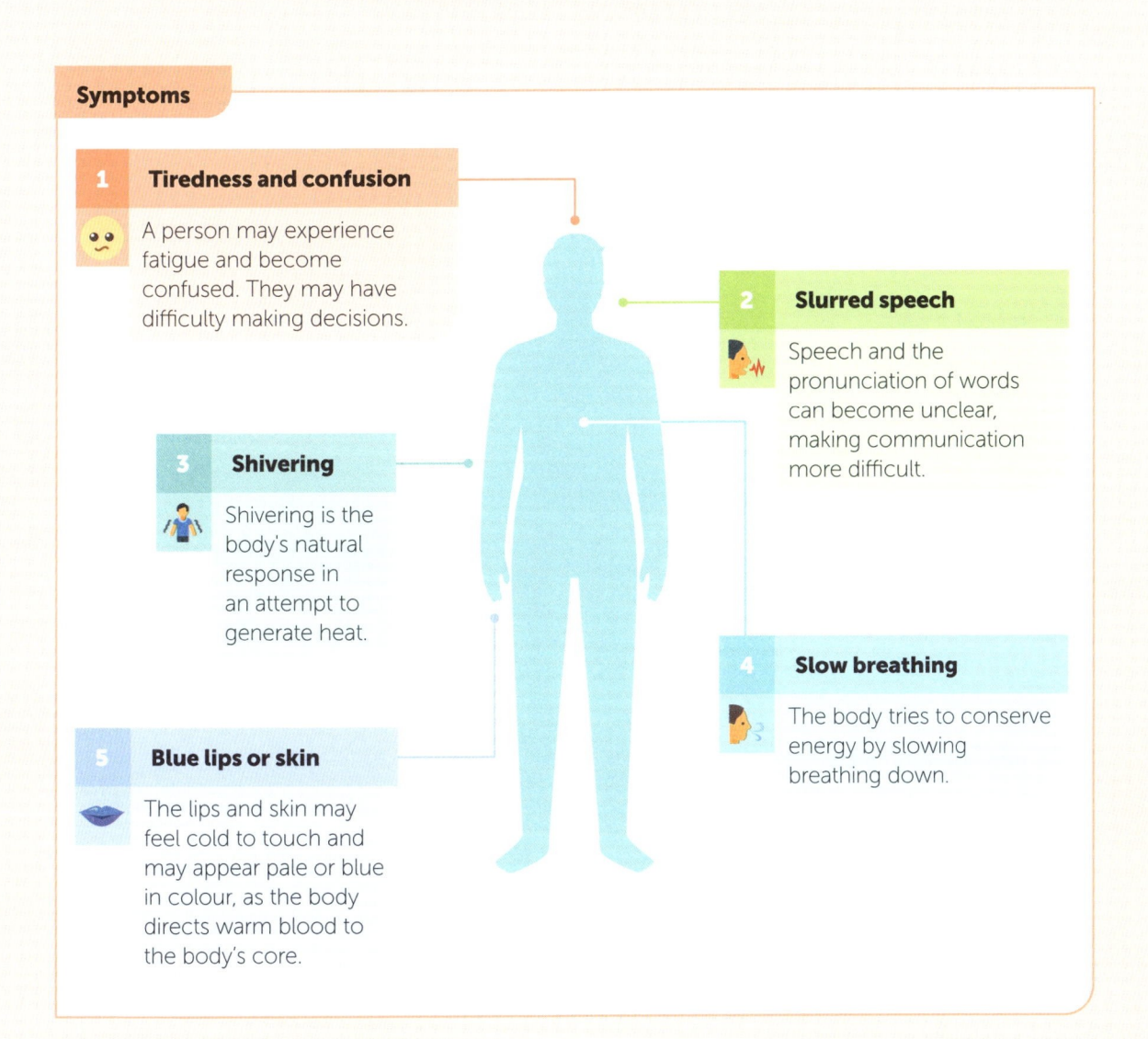

1 Tiredness and confusion
A person may experience fatigue and become confused. They may have difficulty making decisions.

2 Slurred speech
Speech and the pronunciation of words can become unclear, making communication more difficult.

3 Shivering
Shivering is the body's natural response in an attempt to generate heat.

4 Slow breathing
The body tries to conserve energy by slowing breathing down.

5 Blue lips or skin
The lips and skin may feel cold to touch and may appear pale or blue in colour, as the body directs warm blood to the body's core.

Treatment and what to avoid

The treatment for hypothermia involves raising the body temperature to normal range. **Rewarming** a person with hypothermia should be done gradually to avoid complications such as **rewarming shock**. You should never use hot baths or heating devices, such as a hot water bottle, that could cause burns. You should also avoid massaging or rubbing body parts to warm them as it can damage frostbitten areas, draw blood away from the internal organs, and vigorous movements could cause cardiac arrest.

> Rewarming shock is a drop in blood pressure, resulting from too rapid rewarming.

- **Remove wet clothing, wrap in blankets and cover head:** Replace wet clothing with dry, warm clothing. Additionally, wrap the person in warm blankets or a foil survival blanket to help raise their body temperature. Cover the head to help prevent significant heat loss.

- **Provide a warm and sugary non-alcoholic drink:** This will help raise a person's body temperature.

HEAT EXHAUSTION

Heat exhaustion is a condition that arises when the body is unable to cool itself efficiently, often due to prolonged exposure to high temperatures and inadequate fluid intake. This results in an elevated core body temperature.

Causes

Prolonged exposure to extreme heat, worsened by dehydration (see **page 68**), can cause heat exhaustion. If the body is not promptly cooled within 30 minutes, it can progress to a serious condition known as **heat stroke**.

> Heat stroke can lead to organ damage and, in severe cases, can be fatal.

Body temperature of 38°C or above

The normal body temperature is 37°C. If the body gets too hot and the core body temperature rises above 38°C, it can lead to heat exhaustion. A temperature of over 40°C is a sign of heat stroke.

Strenuous physical activity

Engaging in strenuous physical activity in hot conditions, without rest and adequate hydration will increase the risk of heat exhaustion.

Not enough water intake

Insufficient fluid intake or excessive loss of fluids through sweating, without replacing them, can lead to dehydration, reducing the body's ability to cool down.

Symptoms

1. **Excessive sweating:** Excessive sweating is a primary symptom as the body attempts to cool itself down.

2. **Headache / dizziness:** Having a headache is a result of dehydration and increased blood flow to the skin. Heat exhaustion can also cause a drop in blood pressure, leading to feeling dizzy.

3. **Being very thirsty:** This is due to excessive sweating and dehydration.

4. **Feeling or being sick:** Heat exhaustion can lead to feelings of nausea, and in some cases vomiting.

5. **Rapid pulse and / or breathing:** The heart rate will increase as the body works to pump more blood to cool the skin. This also increases an individual's breathing rate.

Treatment

Move to a cool place / cool the skin

A person with heat exhaustion should be removed from the heat immediately and into a cooler environment, ideally with air-conditioning or a shaded area.

Get them to drink plenty of water

The person should drink plenty of cool water. Sports drinks can also be used as **electrolytes** within them can help replace lost fluids.

Electrolytes support fluid absorption, aiding effective rehydration.

---

1. Which **one** of the following is a common symptom of heat exhaustion? [1]
    - A – Absence of sweating
    - B – Excessive shivering
    - C – Increased body temperature
    - D – Reduced pulse rate
2. State **two** preventative measures for heat exhaustion. [2]
3. Compare and contrast heat exhaustion and hypothermia. [4]

---

1. C – Increased body temperature.[1]

2. Avoid prolonged exposure to high temperatures.[1] / Stay well hydrated by drinking fluids regularly.[1]

3. **Similarities:** Both heat exhaustion and hypothermia involve a dysfunction in the body's ability to regulate temperature.[1] / Symptoms of both can include dizziness, confusion, fatigue, and nausea.[1] / Left untreated, both can lead to serious or life-threatening complications.[1]

    Differences: Heat exhaustion occurs when the body's core temperature goes above 38°C and hypothermia goes below 35°C [1] / Heat exhaustion is when the body over heats due to prolonged exposure to high temperature, hypothermia is when the body is exposed to extreme cold temperatures[1] / symptoms of heat exhaustion may include heavy sweating, weakness, rapid pulse whereas symptoms of hypothermia may include shivering, confusion, slurred speech[1] / treatment of heat exhaustion will involve cooling the body, rehydration and rest, whereas hypothermia treatment will include gradual warming, removal of wet clothing, insulation and warming techniques.[1]

OCR Cambridge Nationals **Sport Science – R180: Topic Area 5**

5.5.9–5.5.12

DEHYDRATION

Dehydration is a condition that occurs when the body loses more fluids than it takes in, leading to an insufficient amount of water to support normal bodily functions. Dehydration can also be caused by **diabetes** (see **page 58**).

Causes

Loss of bodily fluids: Various factors contribute to a loss of bodily fluids including insufficient water intake, excessive sweating, vomiting and diarrhoea.

Symptoms

The symptoms of dehydration can vary in severity, and include:

1. **Feeling thirsty:** A strong sensation of thirst is a common early sign of dehydration, signalling that the body needs more fluids.
2. **Fatigue:** Dehydration can lead to a decrease in energy levels and an overall feeling of tiredness.
3. **Dark yellow urine and infrequent urination:** The colour of urine can provide valuable information about a person's hydration level. A clear colour indicates a person is well hydrated, whereas a dark yellow colour indicates a person is dehydrated.
4. **Dry mouth / lips:** Reduced saliva production and lack of moisture in the mouth will cause a dry mouth and lips.

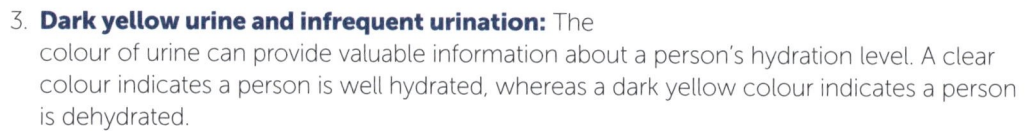

Treatment

The main treatment for dehydration is rehydration. Suggestions for treatment include:

Drink plenty of water

The most obvious thing to do if you have any symptoms of dehydration. **Drink plenty of water** or diluted squash. You should never drink alcohol if you show signs of dehydration.

Use rehydration sachets

Rehydration sachets are powdered formulations containing a combination of electrolytes and glucose that are dissolved in water to create a solution designed to help alleviate dehydration.

How to manage dehydration when participating in sport/exercise

Managing dehydration during sport or exercise is crucial for maintaining performance, preventing heat-related illnesses and ensuring overall well-being. Some ways to do this are:

- Hydrate before exercise
- Monitor sweat loss
- Include electrolytes
- Drink fluids regularly
- Listen to your body
- Adjust fluid intake for the conditions
- Choose the right fluid
- Rehydrate after exercise
- Avoid extreme heat

1. Dehydration affects the colour of urine.
   What colour would you expect urine to be if a person was dehydrated? [1]

   A – Clear
   B – Dark yellow
   C – Pale yellow
   D – Pink

2. State **one** advantage of rehydration sachets over pure water intake after physical activity. [1]

---

1. B – Dark yellow.[1]

2. Rehydration sachets contain electrolytes essential for fluid balance.[1] / Rehydration sachets give a more rapid absorption of fluids in the body.[1]

OCR Cambridge Nationals **Sport Science – R180: Topic Area 5**

Topic Area 5

EXAMINATION PRACTICE

Topic area 5: Causes, symptoms, and treatment of medical conditions

1. Which **one** of the following is a common symptom of asthma? [1]
   - ☐ A – Excessing sweating
   - ☐ B – Headaches
   - ☐ C – Unconsciousness
   - ☐ D – Wheezing

2. Identify **four** symptoms of hypothermia. [4]

3. Draw a straight line to match each medical condition to the correct description. [3]

Medical Condition	Description
Sudden Cardiac Arrest	The body is unable to cool itself efficiently.
Heat exhaustion	The body loses more fluids than it takes in.
Dehydration	The body loses heat faster than it can produce heat.
	The heart suddenly stops beating due to a malfunction with its electrical system.

4. Compare and contrast Type 1 and Type 2 diabetes.
   Consider the age of onset and lifestyle factors in your response. [4]

5. State **two** causes of a sudden cardiac arrest (SCA). [2]

6. A sportsperson has epilepsy.
   (a) Describe **two** common symptoms of an epileptic seizure. [4]
   (b) Explain **one** possible treatment to manage the likelihood of seizures. [2]

70 ClearRevise

7. Which **one** of the following is not a cause of a sudden cardiac arrest? [1]
   - ☐ A – Intense physical activity
   - ☐ B – Sudden trauma
   - ☐ C – Tiredness
   - ☐ D – Underlying genetic heart conditions

8. The Marathon Des Sables is a six-day annual ultramarathon over 250 km of desert terrain across Morocco.

   (a) Explain **one** reason why an athlete with asthma may need to take extra care when competing in a desert ultramarathon. [2]

   (b) Evaluate the preparation necessary for an athlete to be able to complete the race.

   In your response you should consider the advance preparation and management of any issues. [8]

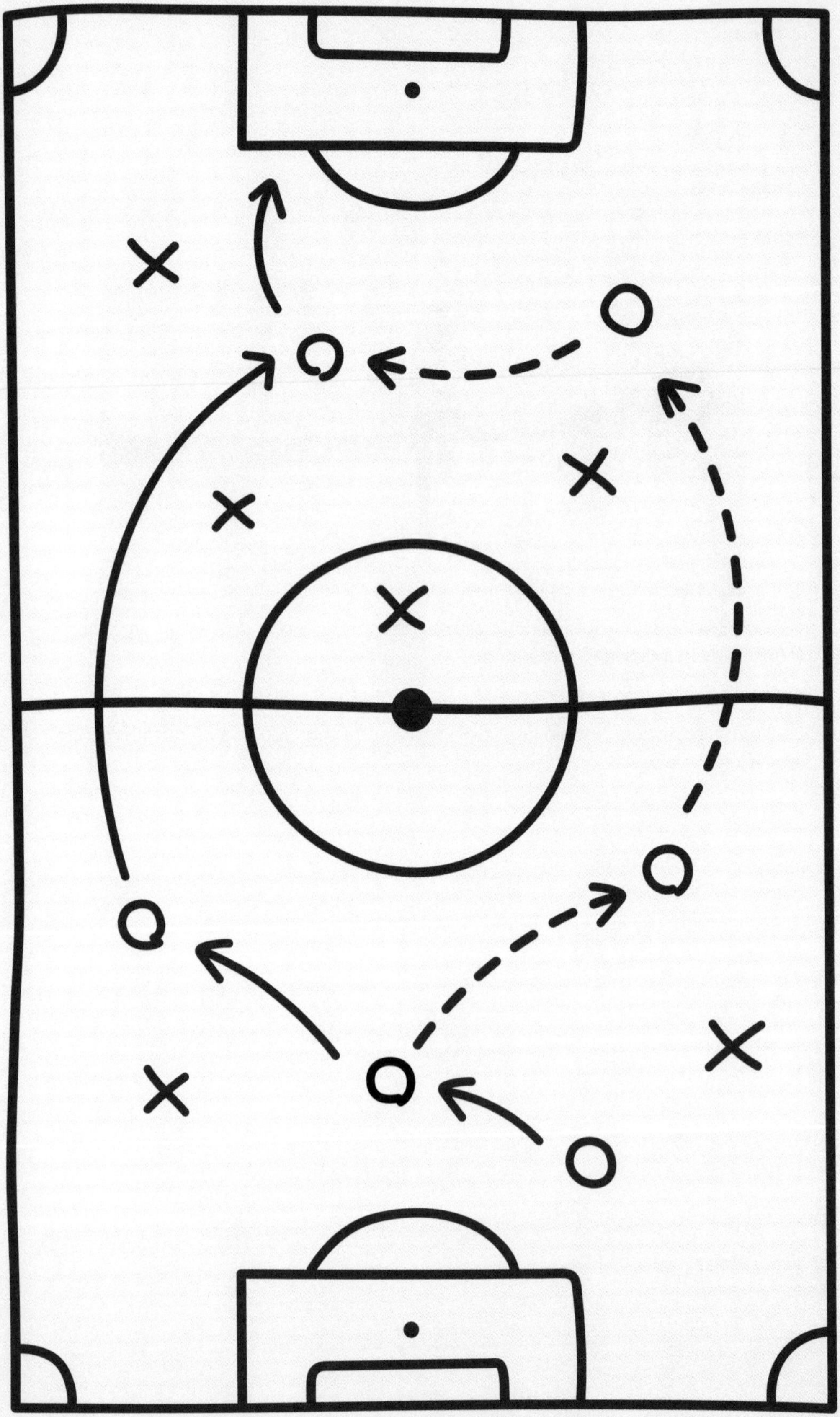

NON-EXAM ASSESSMENT (NEA)

Unit R181: Applying the principles of training: fitness and how it affects skill performance

Information about the non-examined assessment

Assessment
Assessed by teachers, moderated by OCR.
80 marks
40% of the qualification grade

For Unit R181, you'll complete five assessments or tasks in total.

NEA

Task 1 Components of fitness applied in sport (Marks available: 12)

In Task 1, you are required to conduct fitness tests to assess your own level of fitness in **both** of your selected sporting activities, selected from the approved activity list:

Team sports: *Acrobatic gymnastics, association football, badminton, basketball, camogie, cricket, dance, figure skating, futsal, Gaelic football, handball, hockey, hurling, ice hockey, inline roller hockey, lacrosse, netball, rowing, rugby league, rugby union, sailing, sculling, squash, table tennis, tennis, volleyball, water polo.* **Specialist sports:** *blind cricket, goalball, powerchair football, table cricket, wheelchair basketball, wheelchair rugby.*

Individual sports: *Amateur boxing, athletics, badminton, canoeing, cross country running, cycling, dance, diving, equestrian, figure skating, golf, gymnastics, kayaking, rock climbing, sailing, sculling, skiing, snowboarding, squash, swimming, table tennis, tennis, trampoline, windsurfing.* **Specialist sports:** *Boccia, polybat.*

To do this, you must research and select the tests that are appropriate for each of your selected activities, before completing the selected fitness tests and interpret your results data.

- Explain the different tests and their associated components of fitness.
- Include examples that are appropriate for each of your selected sporting activities.
- Explain what the data tells you about your fitness levels in relation to **both** of your selected activities.
- Compare your data to normative data.

Evidence required for Task 1

- Written report or presentation

Task 2 Components of fitness applied in sport (Marks available: 18)

In Task 2, you need to demonstrate which skills within your **two** sporting activities are appropriate to each component of fitness.

To do this, you must research and demonstrate which components of fitness are relevant to skills in **both** activities. Design tests for two main skills you have highlighted in **one** of your selected activities before you complete the tests and collate the results. You must then analyse the data (strengths and weaknesses) from the two tests.

- Include a wide variety of skills that cover the full range of components of fitness.
- Justify which skills are most relevant to your selected activity.
- Make sure your skills tests measure a component of fitness that will improve your performance.

Evidence required for Task 2

- Written report or presentation

Task 3 Principles of training in sport (Marks available: 24)

In Task 3, you need to gather information about the principles of training, training methods and goal setting that include the differences between aerobic and anaerobic exercise, using examples of each.

To do this, you must, discuss how the principles of training and goal setting can be applied to the training programme in the scenario given. You will then need to analyse the benefits of applying the principles to the training programme and each training method, including a comparison of aerobic and anaerobic exercise.

- Research the principles of training (SPOR) and goal setting (SMART) and how they are applied.
- Discuss the training methods in terms of aerobic or anaerobic, intensity, duration, and oxygen consumption for both.
- Know the structure and adaptations of the training methods needed for different components of fitness.
- Apply each element of SMART to your selected activity.

Evidence required for Task 3

- Written report or presentation

Task 4 Organising and planning a fitness training programme (Marks available: 14)

In Task 4, you need to produce and complete a six-week fitness training programme to improve your performance for one of your sporting activities.

To do this, you must, plan and develop a six-week training programme for your selected activity that includes a warm up and cool down, that can be used before and after each session. A risk assessment must also be complete that takes into account the safety considerations.

- The warm up and cool down can be the same each session.
- Ensure the sessions are suitable for your training method.
- Include corrective actions for identified risks.
- Monitor your progress by completing appropriate fitness test(s) at the start and end of your training programme.

Evidence required for Task 4

- Written plan for one specific activity
- Risk assessment – Template provided by OCR.

Task 5 Evaluate own performance in planning and delivery of a fitness training programme (Marks available: 12)

In Task 5, you need to evaluate how your programme went and how it could be improved for the future.

To do this, you must compare fitness test results from before and after the training programme, describe what went well and not so well, how you adapted your plan throughout the programme and the reasons for these adaptations, the effectiveness of the programme and how your plan could be improved in the future.

- Refer to whether the goals set at the start were achieved.
- Make comments on the strengths and areas for improvement of your programme.
- Explain and justify any changes made from your original plan.
- Justify future changes to your plan.

Evidence required for Task 5

- Written report

EXAMINATION PRACTICE ANSWERS

Topic Area 1: Different factors which influence the risk and severity of injury

1. **D** – Motivation. [1]

2. (a) Three from: Gender / age / experience / weight / fitness levels / technique / nutrition / hydration / medical conditions / sleep / previous or recurring injuries. [3]

   (b) Increased fatigue,[1] will decrease the athlete's physical and mental alertness, leading to a greater risk of injury.[1] / Impaired decision making,[1] will affect an athlete's ability to process information quickly, leading to a greater risk of injury. [1] / Reduced recovery,[1] lack of sleep will slow down muscle repair and the release of growth hormones, hindering the body's ability to heal.[1] [2]

3. Two from: Temperature / playing surface / human interaction from other performers / officials / spectators. [2]

4. (a) Mental rehearsal. [1] (b) Fostering a sense of confidence and self-belief. [1] (c) Selective attention. [1] [3]

5. Proper technique ensures efficiency, [1] allowing athletes to execute movements with optimal effectiveness. [1] / Correct technique encourages proper joint and muscle alignment during movements, [1] decreasing the risk of sports injuries. [1] / Constant correct technique promotes long term musculoskeletal health, [1] decreasing the cumulative stress on joints and tissues leading to chronic injuries. [1] [2]

6. High anxiety may lead to muscle tension / impaired decision making / decreased coordination, [1] increasing the risk of injuries through mistimed movements / collisions. [1] [2]

7. Pressure creates a heightened sense of urgency and expectation. [1] Athletes may feel compelled to take more risks / adopt aggressive tactics to meet these external demands. [1] Example: In a football match, players may use forceful tackles and confrontations, driven by the expectations of the coaches and fans. [1] [3]

8. In sport, equipment can enhance athlete performance and help ensure safety. However, there is potential for harm when not used correctly.

   Protective equipment: plays a crucial role in safeguarding athletes during sporting activities. [✓] Designed to reduce the risk and severity of injuries, protective gear such as helmets, pads, and guards [✓] serves as a barrier between the athlete's body and potential impacts. [✓] These items are especially vital in contact sports [✓] like football and hockey. [✓] The significance of protective equipment lies in its ability to absorb and distribute force, [✓] reducing the impact [✓] on vulnerable body parts. When used correctly, protective equipment can significantly help injury prevention, allowing athletes to engage in their respective sports with a reduced likelihood of severe harm. [✓]

   Performance equipment: is used to enhance an athlete's capability [✓] and optimise their performance. [✓] From specialised rackets in tennis to aerodynamic cycling helmets, [✓] the equipment is designed to provide athletes with a competitive edge. [✓] The significance of performance equipment lies in its potential to improve an athlete's skills and overall game. [✓] However, it is essential to emphasise the importance of proper training and supervision [✓] when using performance equipment, as its misuse or overreliance may lead to injuries or reduce the intended benefits. [✓]

   Clothing: serves both functional and protective purposes in sports. [✓] Beyond its role in maintaining comfort and regulating body temperature, [✓] sports clothing can contribute to injury prevention. Compression garments, [✓] for example, provide support to muscles and joints, [✓] reducing the risk of strains and sprains. [✓] Additionally, appropriate clothing can minimise the impact of environmental factors, such as cold or wet conditions. [✓] The significance of sports clothing in athlete safety is highlighted by its ability to enhance performance, aid in injury prevention, and promote overall well-being during sport. [✓]

   Footwear: is a very important part of an athlete's equipment, influencing performance and safety. Proper footwear provides stability, support, and traction, [✓] reducing the risk of slips, trips, and falls. [✓] Different sports require specific types of footwear tailored to the demands of the activity, [✓] whether it's running shoes with proper cushioning or studded football boots for grip on a pitch. [✓] The significance of footwear in athlete safety lies in its ability to prevent common injuries, such as ankle sprains and stress fractures, [✓] by offering the necessary support. However, selecting the wrong type of footwear or neglecting its maintenance can potentially lead to injuries. [✓]

   In conclusion, sports equipment plays a significant role in reducing the risk and severity of injuries in sports when used correctly. [✓]

   This question should be marked in accordance with the levels-based mark scheme on page 82. [8]

Topic Area 2: Warm up and cool down routines

1. **D** – Static stretching. [1]
2. **B** – Light jog. [1]
3. (a) Increase in muscle temperature [1] - improves flexibility and reduces the risk of muscle strains and injuries. [1] / Increase in heart rate [1] - delivering more oxygenated blood to the working muscles. [1] / Increase in flexibility of muscles and joints[1] - contributes to better performance and reduces the risk of injuries. [1] / Increase in pliability of ligaments and tendons [1] - increases the suppleness of connective tissues and reduces muscles stiffness. [1] / Increase in blood flow and oxygen to muscles [1] - helps deliver oxygen and nutrients to the working muscles, preparing them for exercise. [1] / Increase in the speed of muscle contraction [1] - can enhance coordination and reaction time during physical activity. [1] [6]
   (b) Gradually lower heart rate [1] / gradually lower temperature [1] / circulates blood and oxygen [1] / helps prevent blood pooling [1] / gradually reduces breathing rate [1] / removes waste products [1] / reduces risk of DOMS [1]. [3]
   (c) Answers include: (i) Pulse lowering. [1], (ii) – Slow jogging / walking. [1] (iii) – Stretching (maintenance, static or PNF). [1], (iv) – Standing hamstring stretch / shoulder cross body stretch or equivalent. [1] [4]

Topic Area 3: Different types and causes of sports injuries

1. **B** – Long Jump. [1]
2. (a) Tennis elbow / Lateral epicondylitis. [1]
   (b) Repetitive movements / incorrect techniques / overuse of forearm muscles. [1]
   (c) Two from: Ensure proper technique / warm up properly / thorough stretching / strength training / sufficient rest. [2]
3. (a) Bleeding / pain / visible wound. [1] (b) Cleaning / antiseptic / stitches. [1] (c) Fluid filled sac / pain / redness. [1] (d) Avoidance of further friction / bandaging / antiseptic / bandaging. [1] [4]
4. **Causes:** (Tennis elbow) repetitive use of the forearm and wrist, such as in tennis or gripping activities. [1] (Shin splints) overuse and repetitive stress on the shinbone and the tissues attaching the shinbone to the muscles. [1]
   Symptoms: (Tennis elbow) pain on the outer part of the elbow, weak grip strength, tenderness over the outer elbow. [1] (Shin splints) pain along the inner edge of the shin, tenderness, swelling, or soreness on the inner side of the shin, pain during or after exercise. [1]
   Treatments: (Tennis elbow & Shin Splints) rest and activity modifications, ice and anti-inflammatory medications. [1] (Tennis elbow) Physical therapy for strengthening and flexibility, bracing or splinting. [1] (Shin splints) Correct footwear, stretching and strengthening exercise. [1] [4]
5. Indicative content:

   Soft tissue injuries typically involve muscles, tendons, and ligaments. [✓]

   Sprain: *Description:* A sprain is when the ligaments in a joint are overstretched or torn. [✓] *Potential cause:* Could be caused by twisting or rolling an ankle. [✓] In football, an uneven playing surface, [✓] or a sudden change in direction or a bad tackle could cause a player to receive a sprain. [✓] *Symptoms:* symptoms of a sprain include pain, swelling and difficulty bearing weight [✓] on the injured joint. There might also be bruising [✓] around the affected area. *Treatments:* The best course of action for a sprain is protection, rest, ice, compression, and elevation. [✓] A severe sprain may need medical attention and physical therapy. [✓]

   Strain: *Description:* A strain occurs when the muscles or tendons are stretched or torn. [✓] *Potential cause:* In football, a strain injury might be caused by overexertion, improper warm-up, or sudden, forceful movements. [✓] For instance, performing explosive sprints, sudden changes in direction, or attempting powerful kicks [✓] without an appropriate warm up. [✓] *Symptoms:* Common symptoms of a strain include pain, swelling, muscle spasms, and difficulty with the affected muscle's range of motion. [✓] *Treatments:* The recommended treatment for a strain injury involves rest, ice, compression, and elevation. [✓] Rehabilitation exercises can help restore strength and flexibility to the strained muscle. [✓]

   Skin damage: *Description:* Skin damage covers several injuries such as bruises, cuts, grazes, and blisters. [✓] These injures affect the outer most layer of skin, leading to visible damage. [✓] *Potential cause:* Skin damage can result from direct impact with another player or surface, sliding tackles, or friction [✓] between the skin and football boots. [✓] *Symptoms:* Bruises present as discoloured areas, [✓] due to broken blood vessels beneath the skin. [✓] Cuts and grazes cause open wounds with bleeding, [✓] while blisters are fluid filled sacs on the skin's surface. [✓] Pain and tenderness [✓] are common symptoms for all. *Treatments:* immediate treatment for skin damage involves cleaning the affected area. [✓] Bruises can be reduced by applying ice. [✓] Cuts and grazes may require antiseptic cream and blisters should be left intact to protect the delicate skin underneath. [✓]

Hard tissue injuries typically involve bones, and joints. [✓]

Fractures: *Description:* Fractures are broken bones; [✓] they can be open or closed. [✓] Open fractures are when the bone pierces the skin, whereas closed fractures are when the skin is not pierced. [✓] *Potential cause:* In football, fractures can occur in various bones, including the shin, ankle, or collarbone, due to high impact collision, falls, or awkward landings. [✓] Forceful impacts, such as a hard tackle, collisions with another player whilst competing for a header, or a fall after a tackle can result in fractures. [✓] *Symptoms:* Common symptoms include intense pain, swelling, bruising, deformity, and an inability to use or bear weight [✓] on the affected limb. Open fractures will also lead to a loss of blood. [✓] *Treatments:* Immediate medical attention, [✓] immobilise the injured area using splints or braces. [✓] Severe fractures may need surgical operations. [✓] Pain management, rest and rehabilitation exercises are essential to recovery. [✓]

Dislocations: *Description:* A dislocation occurs when the bones that form a joint are forced out of their normal position. [✓] In football, dislocations often involve joints such as the shoulder or finger, [✓] and they can result from falls, collisions, or sudden forceful impacts. [✓] *Potential cause:* In football, a direct blow to a joint from a shoulder barge to try and win a 50/50, [✓] a fall onto an outstretched hand after being tackled from behind, [✓] or a forceful collision with a goalkeeper when you are one on one. [✓] *Symptoms:* Common symptoms of a dislocation include severe pain, swelling, deformity and the inability to move the affected joint. [✓] *Treatments:* Immediate medical attention [✓] is required following a dislocation, where medical professionals will carefully manipulate the bones back into their normal position. [✓] After this, the joint needs to be immobilised with a cast or sling. [✓]

This question should be marked in accordance with the levels-based mark scheme on page 82. [8]

Topic Area 4: Reducing risk, treatment and rehabilitation of sports injuries and medical conditions

1. **D** – Emergency risk. [1]
2. **C** – Massage. [1]
3. **D** – Protection. [1]
4. (a) The purpose of a risk assessment is to identify, analyse, and prioritise risks [1] so that appropriate measures can be taken to ease or manage them effectively [1]. [2]

   (b) Two from: Age of participants [1] as younger or older participants may be more susceptible to injury. [1] / Medical conditions [1] may impact risk if there is a pre-existing condition affected by exercise. [1] / Skill level [1] since less skilled individuals may be more at risk. [1] / Fitness level [1] as this could lead to a greater chance of sprains or heart conditions. [1] / Experience [1] as beginners are more prone to errors or poor technique which can lead to injury. [1]. [4]

   (c) A medical can detect early signs and symptoms of pre-existing conditions [1] to establish an individual's suitability for the intended activity. [1] [2]

5. (a) Assess the person's breathing / Look, listen, and feel for signs of breathing. [1] / If they are not breathing / if breathing is irregular or inadequate [1] initiate rescue breaths if trained to do so. [1] [2]

   (b) The recovery position helps keep an individual's airway clear [1] and allows any fluids (saliva, vomit etc) to drain from the mouth. [1] Placing someone in the recovery position helps to prevent choking and maintain an open airway. [1] [2]

6. Fractures, [1] dislocations, [1] growth plate damage. [1] [2]

7. **See:** Ask if anybody saw what happened and stop the activity immediately, [1] **Active:** – Ask the injured person if they can move the injured area, [1] **Passive:** Gently move the injured limb or joint through the full range of movement. [3]

8. (a) Exposure to extremely cold temperatures to reduce inflammation and promote healing [1]. (b) Pain relief, reduced swelling, accelerated recovery, and improved muscle function [1]. (c) Medications such as Ibuprofen, to alleviate pain and manage inflammation [1]. (d) Temporary relief from pain, improved comfort during rehabilitation, and enhanced ability to participate in therapeutic exercises [1]. [4]

9. Hot and cold therapies are commonly employed in the treatment of sports injuries, each serving distinct purposes in managing pain, inflammation, and promoting recovery. [✓] The choice between these treatments depends on the nature of the injury.

   Similarities: Both hot and cold therapies aim to alleviate pain and enhance the healing process. [✓] They are cost-effective, non-invasive methods [✓] that can be easily administered at home or in a medical setting. [✓] The application, frequency and duration should be monitored [✓] to prevent negative effects.

Differences: Cold Therapy is primarily used in the acute phase [✓] of injuries to reduce swelling, inflammation, and numb pain. [✓] Cold constricts blood vessels, slowing down blood flow to the injured area, [✓] thereby reducing swelling and numbing pain. [✓] Examples of use would be to treat initial injuries immediately following a sprain, strain, or impact injury. [✓] Hot Therapy is generally applied during the longer phases of injuries [✓] to enhance blood flow, relax muscles, and alleviate stiffness. [✓] Heat dilates blood vessels, improving circulation [✓] and promoting the delivery of oxygen and nutrients to the injured area. [✓] Examples of use would be to treat muscle stiffness. [✓]

Advantages: *Prior to performance* – Cold Therapy will reduce muscle soreness and inflammation, potentially preventing injury [✓]. Hot therapy will increase blood flow and relax muscles, enhancing flexibility. [✓]
During performance – Cold therapy can be applied briefly to manage acute injuries or reduce pain, e.g., using an ice pack on a minor sprain. [✓] Hot therapy will not typically be used during performance due to the risk of overheating. [✓]
Immediately after injury – Cold therapy will control inflammation and minimise swelling, reducing pain and potential tissue damage. [✓] Hot therapy will promote blood flow, which aids in the removal of waste products and facilitates the healing process. [✓]
As part of the longer-term rehabilitation process – Cold therapy will manage inflammation during the recovery phase, facilitating the healing process and aiding in pain management. [✓] Hot therapy will relax muscles, helping to improve range of motion and decrease stiffness during rehabilitation exercises. [✓]

In conclusion, the choice between hot and cold therapies depends on the type of the injury and the stage of the healing process. [✓] Cold therapy is advantageous for acute injuries to reduce inflammation, [✓] while hot therapy is more suitable for chronic conditions to enhance blood flow and promote muscle relaxation. [✓]

This question should be marked in accordance with the levels-based mark scheme on page 82. [8]

Topic Area 5: Causes, symptoms, and treatment of medical conditions

1. **D** – Wheezing. [1]

2. Shivering [1] / blue lips or skin [1] / slurred speech [1] / tiredness or confusion [1] / slowed breathing [1]. [4]

3. **Sudden Cardiac Arrest** – When the heart suddenly stops beating due to a malfunction with its electrical system. [1]
   Heat Exhaustion – When the body is unable to cool itself efficiently. [1]
   Dehydration – When the body loses more fluids than it takes in. [1] [3]

4. **Age of onset** – Type 1 diabetes is often diagnosed in childhood or adolescence [1] / Type 2 diabetes is often diagnosed in adulthood but can occur in youth. [1]
   Lifestyle factors – Type 1 diabetes is generally not linked to lifestyle factors such as obesity or a sedentary lifestyle [1] / Type 2 diabetes has a strong correlation with lifestyles choices such as obesity, physical inactivity, or poor diet habits. [1] [4]

5. Two from: underlying genetic heart condition,[1] / intense physical activity,[1] / sudden trauma.[1] [2]

6. (a) Eyes [1] can start staring blankly / fluttering / rapid blinking.[1] Mouth, [1] biting tongue / random noises. [1] Limbs [1] can experience stiffness / jerking movements. [1] [4]

   (b) Anti-epileptic drugs / (AEDs) [1] help to manage the chemical levels in the brain [1] which may lessen seizures. Ketogenic diet [1] introduces a high fat, low carbohydrate diet that changes the chemical levels in the brain. [1] [2]

7. **C** – Tiredness. [1]

8. (a) Environmental conditions (hot / dusty / dry air) / intense exercise [1] may act as a trigger / cause an attack. [1] [2]

   (b) Preparing for the Marathon Des Sables requires meticulous planning. Preparation necessary for an athlete, considering both advance preparation and the management of potential issues could include:

   Advance preparation:

   Nutritional planning: *Hydration strategies:* Given the desert environment, developing effective hydration [✓] strategies is critical. Athletes must practice drinking the required amount of water to prevent dehydration. [✓] Athletes must carry sufficient water and hydration sachets. [✓] *Nutrition:* Plan and practice the consumption of energy-rich foods suitable for sustained endurance efforts [✓] in extreme conditions. These should be energy dense and portable foods. This is especially important for those with diabetes. [✓]

   Equipment familiarisation: *Backpack training:* Athletes should train with the race-required backpack, [✓] ensuring they are comfortable carrying essentials such as water, food, and mandatory gear. [✓] *Footwear:* Testing and selecting appropriate footwear for desert conditions is vital to prevent blisters and injuries. [✓]

   Mental conditioning: *Mental toughness:* Training should include mental conditioning to handle the physical and psychological challenges of the race, including isolation, fatigue, and self-doubt. [✓] Visualisation techniques and mental rehearsal can be beneficial. [✓] *Problem-solving skills:* Athletes should practice adapting to unexpected situations, such as extreme temperatures or navigation challenges. [✓]

Medical preparedness: *Sports injuries:* Carry a well-equipped medical kit [✓] and ensure the participant has sufficient knowledge of basic first aid. [✓] *Medical conditions:* Carrying sufficient supplies of personal medication and have an understanding for specific health conditions. [✓]

Management of issues:

Medical checkups: *Pre-race health assessment:* Athletes should undergo thorough medical checkups to identify any pre-existing conditions or potential risks. [✓] *On-site medical support:* The MdS should have medical professionals on-site, [✓] but athletes should be aware of basic first aid and self-care measures. [✓]

Hydration and nutrition during the race: *Hydration stations:* Plan and utilise hydration stations strategically along the route to maintain fluid balance. [✓] *Nutrition management:* Regular intake of energy gels, snacks, and hydration sachets during the race [✓] is crucial to prevent depletion and maintain energy levels. [✓]

Foot care: *Blister management:* Athletes should carry blister care supplies [✓] and know how to address foot issues promptly. [✓] *Shoe adjustment:* If footwear issues arise, athletes should be prepared to adjust or modify their shoes during the race. [✓]

Adaptation to climate: *Temperature management:* Athletes need strategies to cope with extreme temperatures, [✓] including clothing choices and cooling techniques. [✓]

Race logistics: *Rest and recovery:* Incorporate planned rest and recovery periods [✓] into the race strategy to avoid burnout. [✓]

Medical conditions: *Asthma:* Regular monitoring and management of asthma symptoms. [✓] Use of prescribed inhalers as a preventative measure. [✓] *Diabetes:* Continuous blood glucose monitoring, [✓] adequate insulin management and intake of glucose sources for quick energy. [✓] *Epilepsy:* Compliance with prescribed medications and avoidance of triggers that may induce seizures. [✓] *Sudden cardiac arrest:* Ensure access to AED. [✓] *Hypothermia:* Extreme cold in the dessert at night so layered clothing for insulation [✓] and staying dry and protected from the wind (at night). [✓] *Heat exhaustion:* Adequate hydration [✓] to prevent dehydration, wearing of light, breathable clothing. [✓] *Dehydration:* Regular intake of water and hydration sachets. Monitoring of urine colour for hydration status. [✓]

In conclusion, successful participation in the Marathon Des Sables demands a comprehensive and well-executed preparation plan. [✓] Athletes must focus not only on physical conditioning [✓] but also on mental resilience [✓] and logistical considerations to navigate the challenges of the desert ultramarathon.

This question should be marked in accordance with the levels-based mark scheme on page 82. [8]

LEVELS-BASED MARK SCHEME FOR EXTENDED RESPONSE QUESTIONS

What are extended response questions?

Extended response questions are worth eight marks. These questions are likely to have command words such as 'assess' or 'evaluate'. You need to write in continuous **prose** when you answer one of these questions. This means you must write in full sentences (rather than in bullet points), organised into paragraphs if necessary.

You may need to bring together skills, knowledge and understanding from two or more areas of the specification. To gain full marks, your answer needs to be logically organised, with ideas linked to give a sustained line of reasoning.

Example level descriptors

Level descriptors vary depending on the quality of the response. Level 3 is the highest level and Level 1 is the lowest level. No marks are awarded for an answer with no relevant content. The table gives examples of the typical features that examiners are asked to look for in the eight-mark questions. Once a level has been determined for an answer, an examiner will justify if the response is at the top, middle or bottom of that mark range to determine a final mark for the question.

Level	Mark	Description
0	0	No rewardable content.
1	1–3	Demonstrates isolated knowledge and understanding, there will be major gaps or omissions. Few of the points made will be relevant to the context in the question. Limited assessment which contains generic assertions rather than considering the factors or events and their relative importance, leading to judgements which are superficial or unsupported.
2	4–6	Demonstrates some accurate knowledge and understanding, with only minor gaps or omissions. Some of the points made will be relevant to the context in the question, but the link will not always be clear. Displays a partially developed assessment which considers some of the factors or events and their relative importance leading to partially supported judgements.
3	7–8	Demonstrates mostly accurate and thorough/detailed knowledge and understanding. Most of the points made will be relevant to the context in the question, and there will be clear links. Displays a well-developed and logical assessment which clearly considers the factors or events and their relative importance, leading to supported judgements.

NOTES, DOODLES AND EXAM DATES

Doodles

Exam date

INDEX

A
ability 11
abrasions 32
accidents 5
achilles tendonitis 38
acute injury 29, 49
age 10
aggression 14
airway 47
Alzheimer's disease 35
Anterior Cruciate Ligament (ACL) 31
anti-epileptic drugs (AEDs) 61
anxiety 12
arousal 12
arousal levels 22
asthma 56
Astro pitches 6
Automated External Defibrillator (AED) 63

B
biomechanical issues 36
blisters 33
blood
  glucose 58
  pooling 26
body weight 10
breathing 47
breathing rate 26
bruises 32

C
Cardiopulmonary Resuscitation (CPR) 47
cardio-respiratory system 20
channelled aggression 14
chronic injuries 36
circulation 47
closed fractures 34
clothing 9
coaching 4
communication 4
components of fitness 75
concentration 22
concussion 35
confidence 13, 22
contact sports 2
contrast therapy 51, 52
contusions 32
cool down 24
cryotherapy 51, 52
cuts 32

D
defibrillators 63
dehydration 68
delayed onset muscle soreness (DOMS) 27
dementia 35
diabetes 58
direct aggression 14
dislocations 34, 50
DRABC 47
dynamic stretching 19, 20, 25

E
electrolytes 67
electrotherapy 51, 52
Emergency
  Action Plan (EAP) 45
  communication 45
  personnel 45
endorphins 51
environment 6
epicondylitis 39
epilepsy 60
equipment 8, 45
ethical standards 5
experience 4, 10
extrinsic factors 2

F
first aid 45
first responders 45
fitness levels 10
flexibility 19
focus 22
fog 6
footwear 9
fractures 34, 50

G
gender 10
golfers' elbow 39
grazes 32
group size 43
growth plates 50

H
hazards 42
head injuries 35
heart rate 26
heat 6
  exhaustion 66
  stroke 66
hooliganism 7
hydration 11
hydrotherapy 51, 52
hyperglycaemia 58
hypoglycaemia 58
hypothermia 64

I
imagery 16
immobilisation 51, 52
impact and pain 29
individual variables 10
inhalers 57
injury 3, 5, 8, 11, 29
  acute 40, 49
  chronic 36, 40
  head 35
  soft and hard tissue 30
instructing 4
insulin 59
intrinsic factors 10
isometric muscle contraction 25

K
ketogenic diet 61

L

lacerations 32
lactic acid 27
lateral epicondylitis 39
leading 4
level of risk 42
ligaments 31
litter 6

M

maintenance stretches 24
massage 51, 52
medial epicondylitis 39
medical 44
　conditions 11
mental
　rehearsal 16, 23
　strategies 16
mobility 18
motivation 12, 22
musculoskeletal system 20

N

National Governing Body (NGB) 44
nebulisers 57
non-contact sports 2
nutrition 11

O

officials 7, 15
open fractures 34
overuse 36

P

painkillers 51, 52
paramedics 45
patellar tendonitis 38
performance enhancing drugs (PEDs) 15
performance equipment 8
personnel 45
physiological benefits 20, 26
PRICE 49, 53
Proprioceptive Neuromuscular Facilitation (PNF) 25
protective equipment 8
psychological
　benefits 22
　factors 12
pulse
　lowering 24
　raising 18

R

rain 6
recovery position 48, 52
referees 7
regulations 4
rehydration 68
repetitive movements 37
retaliation 15
rewarming 65
risk assessment 42
rotator cuff tendonitis 38
rules 4

S

safety checks 42
SALTAPS 46
screening 44
seizures 60
selective attention 16
shin splints 40
shivering 65
shock 65
skill rehearsal phase 19
skin damage 32
sleep 11, 60
slurred speech 60, 65
soft tissue injuries 30
spectators 7
sports activity 2
sprains 31, 49
static stretching 25
strains 31, 49
stress 12
stress fractures 40
stretchers 45
stretching 19, 24
Sudden Cardiac Arrest (SCA) 62
supervision 5
support 51, 52

T

technique 4, 11
temperature 26
　conditions 6
tendonitis 38
tendons 31
tennis elbow 39
training 75
trauma 29

U

ultrasound 51, 52

W

warm up 18, 20, 22
weather 6
weight 10
wheezing 56

X

X-rays 50, 52

THE HUMAN SKELETON

Label the major joints and bones on the diagram below. Include the common injuries to occur at each point.

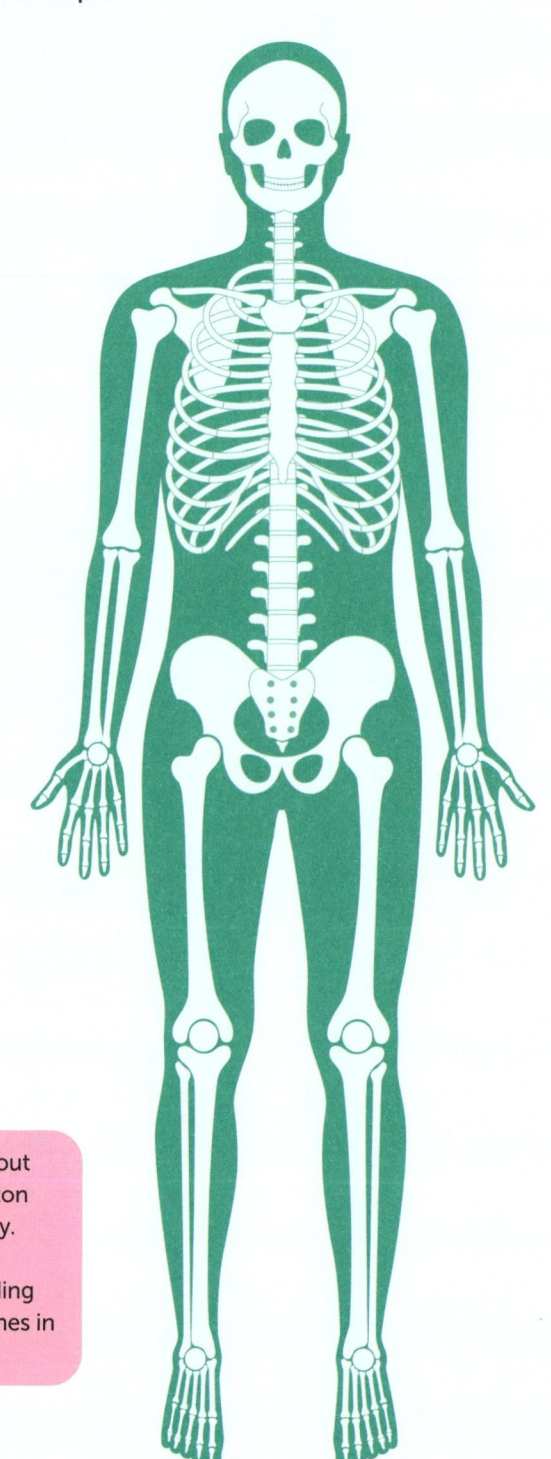

Infants are born with about 270 bones in their skeleton to provide extra flexibility. During childhood, many bones fuse together ending up with typically 210 bones in the adult skeleton.

EXAMINATION TIPS

When you practice examination questions, work out your approximate grade using the following table. This table uses a rounded approximation of boundaries for this qualification. Be aware that boundaries vary for each exam series by a few percentage points either side of those shown.

	\multicolumn{4}{c}{Level 2}	\multicolumn{3}{c}{Level 1}
Grade	Distinction*	Distinction	Merit	Pass	Distinction	Merit	Pass
Code	2*	D2	M2	P2	D1	M1	P1
Boundary	90%	80%	70%	60%	50%	40%	30%

1. Be prepared with a black pen and a ruler.
2. Read each question carefully. Make sure you understand what the question is asking and follow the instructions. You cannot get marks for giving an answer to a question you think is appearing rather than the actual question.
3. Avoid simply rewriting the question or repeating examples that are already given in the question.
4. *Identify*, *outline* and *state* questions require you to recall a short piece of key information. No explanation is required. There will be one mark for each point you make.
5. Remember that *explain* questions have two marks. You need to make a point for the first mark, and then expand this point with a linked development for the second mark. To help you develop your responses, aim to include words such as 'because' or 'therefore'.
6. There is one long answer question on the exam paper worth 8 marks and could use the command verbs *analyse*, *discuss*, or *evaluate*. Remember that the answers to these questions need both advantages and disadvantages. An '*evaluate*' question also needs a conclusion.
7. Answer questions in the spaces provided. If this is not possible e.g. due to deleting a wrong answer, indicate the location of the corrected answer on the paper (e.g. '*see next page*' or '*my answer is on the last blank page*').
8. Do not use the space allocated for answers to write plans for your answers, and do not add extra pages to your answer book with plans/scribbles/items that will not be marked.
9. Don't spend too much time on one question or leave any questions unanswered. If you have time left at the end, check your answers and make any corrections.
10. Before you hand in your paper, read over your answers and check for any mistakes or gaps.
11. Make sure your handwriting is clear and legible.
12. Cross out any errors neatly.
13. Don't let your nerves get the better of you. Remember that you have prepared well, and you can do this.
14. Lastly, try to relax, breathe deeply and focus on the task at hand. Don't compare yourself to others or worry about what they are doing.

Good luck!

New titles coming soon!

These guides are everything you need to ace your exams and beam with pride. Each topic is laid out in a beautifully illustrated format that is clear, approachable and as concise and simple as possible.

They have been expertly compiled and edited by subject specialists, highly experienced examiners, industry professionals and a good dollop of scientific research into what makes revision most effective. Past examination questions are essential to good preparation, improving understanding and confidence.

- Hundreds of marks worth of examination style questions
- Answers provided for all questions within the books
- Illustrated topics to improve memory and recall
- Specification references for every topic
- Examination tips and techniques
- Free Python solutions pack (CS Only)

Absolute clarity is the aim.

Explore the series and add to your collection at **www.clearrevise.com**

Available from all good book shops

amazon   @pgonlinepub

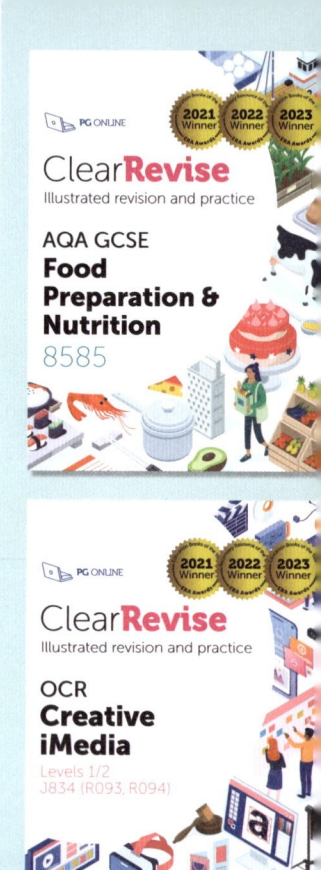

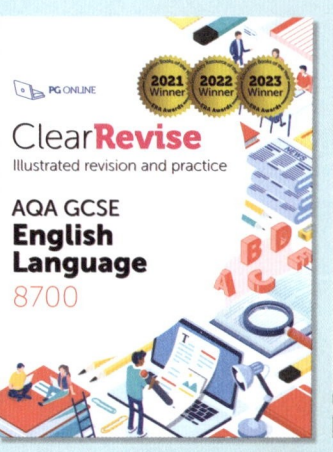

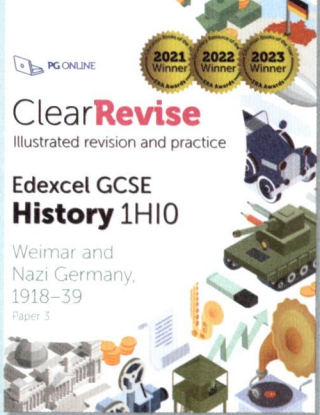

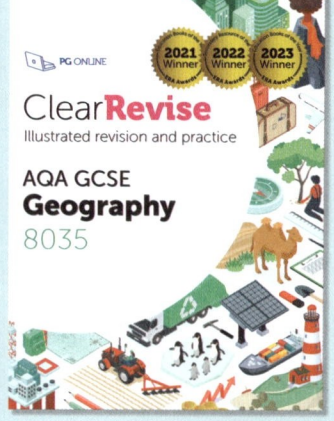

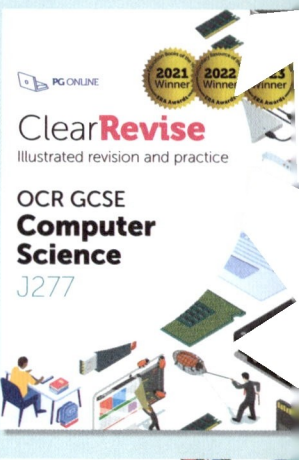

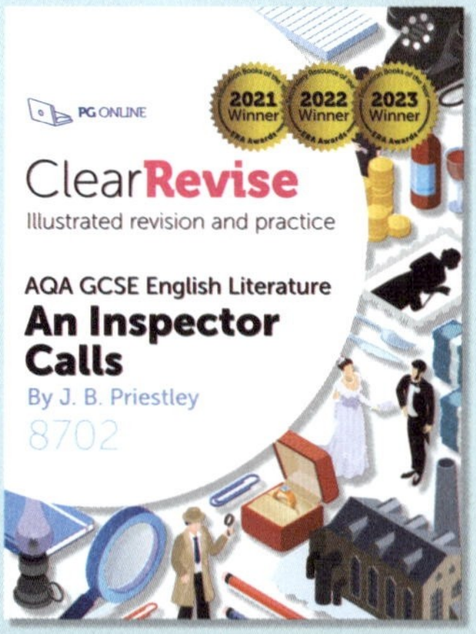

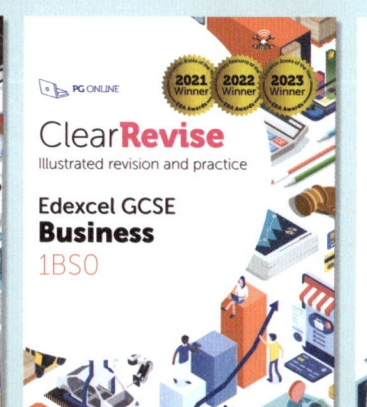

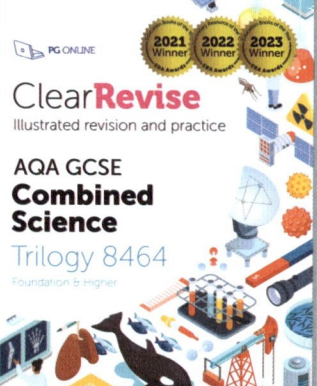

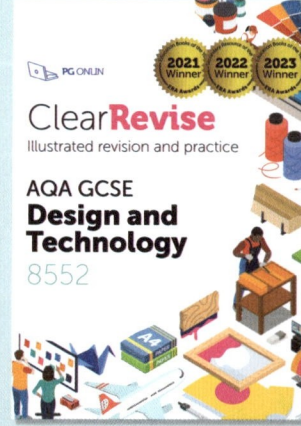